An Inspirational True Story

WHO REALLY WANTS

MONEY?

ISBN 979-8-8691-4329-7

Table of Contents

Dedicated to my mom, Madre

J. T. WILLIAMS

DEVELOPER OF

WATERFALL COUNTRY CLUB &

EAGLES LANDING COUNTRY CLUB

This is a great book from a marvelous young man. I am proud to be his mentor and personally have watched him mature in business, spiritual and moral stands. Men are measured by how many people they influence for the better and not the amount of money in their pocket. This book is for generations, both current and in the future.

J. T. Williams

Madre, Mom, Ms. Sonya

Madre Mom, Ms. Sonya
The day you passed away, your sister called your
name multiple times, I wanted you to say
something
I never believed in the ghost of Christmas past but,
I was wishing to God and Halley's comets
Reminiscing on blissful moments
In shock, and started missing you, your name I will
spiritually honor
It has been too many deaths happening this summer
since you left, too painful to number
Ignoring calls and text messages, I am telling you,
it is always something
I am reaching for better moments in negativity, you
know I can hardly function
I am going through a lot still trying to provide for a
company and multiple countries
But like stated in Rebirth in negative situation
something positive is still accomplished
Madre, Mom, Ms. Sonya
You know me better than most, can you tell that I
am lost?

Can you tell by how I walk, I don't know who to go to, nor how to talk?
Me and my siblings, we just fought, I thought we would figure it out
And literally I am baffled I am still lost
I do not know what the hostility is about
Normally I would call you and rant……..this time I can't
My bursts of anger to you look like I was still a child pouting, to prove I was serious I would tell you. I doubt me and my siblings' relationships with each other will go back to being genuine again
I will give their seats to their kids and that's even when
They say my bad, Simeon!
……..In the softest of voices, I can hear you say "oh boy, here you go again. I understand how you feel but you have to be the bigger person and don't play victim.
Yes, turn the other chin and don't bring it up again"
I would introduce you to my successful friends to see you smile again and hear you say "I knew God spared you for a reason
I hope I could see you live your purpose while I'm still breathing"
…….I remember your tone changing to Simeon I know that I'm leaving

To God, I was constantly pleading but everything in life happens for a reason
And know my heart bleeding, but I'm constantly working and grieving
Healing and peeling back my scabs every time I replace a tear with a laugh
Asking God to put me on the right path till the day we cross paths

-Simeon Nunnally

<u>What's Your Purpose?</u>

I asked the trees, around the time it drops its leaves
 What's your purpose?…..What's your purpose?
 What's your purpose?
Just like you
I sit outside and see beautiful views
Clouds in my peripheral
In the distance ocean, I see deep color blue hues
White spot and dimples seen visible during the
different phases of the moon
    What's your purpose?…..What's your purpose?
    What's your purpose?……..
Because I know it has a purpose, too
No, I'm not perfect like you
Whoever spent the time designing the moon
The time designing the trees
Delicately, swiftly, and perfectly gave order to the
breeze
And order the seas not to seize the land
But stay back 100 feet
Understood said the water
And the oceans humbly agreed

to the point were hurricanes need your permission
to breathe
…..No I'm not that perfect
But since everything has its purpose
I want to know what's my purpose because I'm far
from perfect
But I know my imperfections perfectly fit in your
model of perfection
It took a long time for me to understand that lesson
That even my imperfections are a blessing
At the end of life, hopefully, we will see you in
heaven
I will see my mother and embrace life's seconds
blessings
Because it has to be more to life than sacrifice and
investing
Maybe it is to prove to God we have the discipline
to live forever
in heaven
…….in Heaven

-Simeon H. Nunnally

12

"The Art of Storytelling, when completed in the correct fashion, allows the mind to exercise, through a process known as critical thinking. Critical thinking is the gateway to wisdom and the understanding of life itself."

-Simeon H. Nunnally

Chapter 1
"What is the Reason"?

Another night driving through the boisterous heartbeat known as the Great City of Atlanta. Every sense was stimulated, and I could not help but smile at the fact that the city was truly alive. The nightlife in Atlanta burst with the most contagious, alluring, and welcoming energy, waiting to congratulate you after a successful week. The streets are littered with Mercedes Benz G-Wagons, Land Rovers, Tesla's and my favorite the Lamborghini SUV's. To add to the array of communal noises of friends coming out of pubs and dive bars, smoking cigars while laughing and waiting at streetlights, couples holding hands as they entered restaurants, taking pictures while stealing quick kisses and intimate touches. The gourmet smells of the best steakhouse and French bakeries wafting through the air. It is a beautiful evening driving past Lenox Train Station and the Buckhead Club on my left, to turn right on Lenox

Ave, passing Lenox Mall. I was cruising through the familiar streets of Buckhead, Georgia, as is often the case. I was coming home after a long day of exhausting, yet successful and lucrative meetings with partners and colleagues, meaningful conference calls and rounds of golf with international investors, diplomats, and prospective clients. It was another successful day.

Being a Georgia native, and my extensive familiarity of the roads that I drove down blindly and inherently from routine, each day, I felt a nagging sense of dread and detachment from the lush and opulent neighborhood and surroundings I have worked so hard to be part of. Upon turning into my residential private garage, I came to the closed gate. I pressed the buzzer to allow the arm to rise, and to allow myself entrance into the parking deck. While thinking to myself, "I am extremely thankful for the successes of these projects". I continued to drive into my parking spot that is assigned to my residence. I took a second in the driver's seat to prepare for what would be awaiting me at the top floor of my spacious and extremely well-lit, with natural light, two-bedroom condo. The abrupt sound of the car engine came to a stop, and in doing so, succeeded in swallowing my thoughts and realizations. Silence!

I sighed and hoisted myself out of the driver's seat. I grabbed my caramel brown suit jacket and laptop, locked my car doors, and made the trudge towards the resident's-only private elevator. The sole and deafening echo of my dark brown dress shoes on the garage floor reminded me again of this solitude and isolation that success begets. The elevator ride to the top floor caused a cognitive dissonance within me, for I felt that the elevator ride up was too fast and way too slow.

As I used my remote-less key to enter my home, the stainless-steel kitchen and marble island that I worked so hard for, only provided a cold void of any life, movement, touch, family, noise, or warmth. The vibrant noises of the city, and the sudden burst of laughter from friends hanging out at the local street pubs and adjacent rooftops, could be heard through the stunning panoramic floor-to-ceiling windows which could be found throughout my condo. I set my keys down on the kitchen counter and the noise of the keys hitting the marble stone would ricochet and echo against the walls and throughout my minimally designed and furnished foyer. The smell of sandalwood and vanilla diffused throughout my home, no longer caused me the familiarity and comfort expected of it, instead proved a torturous reiteration and reminder of this singular incessant and uninterrupted sense of scent … for this place, this home, this beautiful box in the sky … lacked the presence of another, a family, children or a loved one, just a reminder of the deepest of losses, my mother. There was no combining of a lover's perfume oil being rubbed into her skin after a hot bath, or the stickiness and smell of freshly baked cinnamon rolls and frosting being licked by my daughter as she guarded the oven stoically and excitedly, waiting for the reward of her work. Or, the smell of my wife cooking my favorite dish as I held her from the back, and hummed our favorite songs spilling from the Bluetooth speakers fixed throughout our home. Instead, it was only the realization of my lone reflection against the glass windows overlooking a city that impassioned me to the same success that propelled me in a conundrum of silence and stark contrast between the life one believes that success would beget, yet the isolation and trials that said success would affect.

You see, if I walk into a bank right now and withdraw $1,000,000 cash and spread the one million dollars all over the wood floors of my home, it would not dull the solitude of success… it would not dull the noise caused by the silence of this involuntary seclusion of ambition and grit. Yet, at what cost or valuation? For, these one million dollars would be incapable of conversing with me, dancing in my arms, giving me an orgasm, cooking with me and for me, wash dishes for me, nor would it be able to give me a back massage saturated with love, tenderness, care, a lover's foreplay, and intimacy. On the contrary, the one million dollars would breed a sleuth of unwanted attention every time I spend a penny of the money.

In truth, the IRS will want their rightful cut, my friends and family will feel entitled to money not acquired or personally obtained, and as biblically and statutorily mandated by faith, the church will want their 10 percent in tithes. Again, this is not what we think about when we are climbing proverbial ladders and seeking what we have convinced ourselves to be the "American Dream". Yet, who really wants to deal with that? To even achieve this idea of wealth and success, one must really believe and really be determined to work effortlessly day and night, in order to one day eat and enjoy the fruits of their labor.

Ultimately, I would achieve wealth after years of training and years of hard work. I grew from every trial which became motivation and I learned how to wield and use motivation in my favor. I would lose close friends and sever familial relationships, yet true to form, God would replace those friends and familiar ties, with angels he would assign and charge to my life. It is this constant covering that my faith and relationship with God would prove as a continual blessing on my path of purpose, and during the journey to live an accomplished life as prescribed by my ministry set forth by my God.

Yet, on this path, I obtained less sleep the more I grew. That part was not enjoyable, but I managed to locate the joys that came with the trials and triumphed over professional obstacles. God blessed me and I came out partially unscathed. In other words, I got a divorce on this road to success and antiquated glory. I missed invaluable opportunities to have quality time with my beautiful daughter. I would miss the birthday parties and celebrations of my nieces and my nephew. Worst of it all, I missed precious moments and sharing time with my mother; for what? All for an inanimate object called money, which in the end, its tangibility and final acquirement can neither acknowledge nor name any of my many sacrifices that I made in order to obtain its inanimate existence.

So, in retrospect, I have come to the full conclusion and understanding that people do not really want money. What they want, instead, is the popularity and stigma associated and assigned to the idea and notion of having money. The false sense of feeling the invincibility through limitless resources. They want to fit in and be accepted by society and promote their vanity. They want to fit in and in a sense, "keep up with the Joneses" when they fail to realize that the "Joneses", are not a fan of them. They are trying to keep up with people who do not admire them. The seeking of money comes about as they want to somehow be empowered and validated by societal pressures and appearances. Societal discourse comes into perspective when the mass majority of the population fall to the gimmick that money solves all problems. The gimmick is the exchange of time away from family for the pursuit money. Where is the balance? In my many years of training, sacrifices, and time invested, I have now realized that the following of such societal discourses, norms, goals, and aspirations has falsely portrayed the model of success and achievement. Thus, I say, be happy and make purpose your driven goal. I say you continuously endeavor to pray and ask God to incessantly guide and direct you to your assigned purpose in life and find happiness. In truth, it is the finding of purpose that is the ultimate goal of success and achievement, and through such optimistic lens and foundational compasses, or morality and integrity, it is that one finds purpose. The wealth that flows from the finding of purpose is organic, well-deserved, and divinely ascertained. The pursuit of money is frivolous and unfounded as it could lead you to losing your identity and compromising your morals to achieve the highest amount satisfiable to one's desires. High stress for high pay is not an even exchange.

If you didn't have any bills to pay and you were able to purchase and ascertain any and every desired material object, home, car, property in life, would you still want money? Would money prove to be enough to satisfy all instinctive, natural and biological urges that we often at times feel, founded on the basis and exuberance of genuine love. The one thing that we all innately yearn for and crave is genuine love and the understanding of individual purpose. Who am I, and why am I here? For you see, you could never be truly satisfied at the mere prospect of "only" having money, because too many questions in your life would go unanswered, and so much of yourself would be unfulfilled. The idea of "all I need is money and that is it" is not a true statement after all. You would want a wife, or a husband, and even children to fill the homes that you so ardently endeavored to obtain. You would want to paint your daughter's nails and play football with your son. You would want to know who created the sun and how was it designed, and what was one thinking when they created the sun. You would want to know who created the moon, and who put the clouds in the sky, and share those ideas with your children. As with or without money, these are still the things that the heart desires. Purpose, community, connection, consistency …. And love.

What is the point of obtaining the world, and losing your soul? Partially meaning, what is the point of obtaining the world and losing your family? What is the point of chasing money and you telling your children you must miss yet another basketball game or ballet recital, due to having to work the overtime necessary to feed, clothe and shelter them? Children in their innocence are unable to understand the full breadth of sacrifices endured for his or her betterment. They in turn have kids of their own and tell their children you were absent at their games and they remember how it feels.

Now as the sacrificial parent, you ultimately warp into a tangible life lesson to the child, and inadvertently teach them, that the pursuit of money lit your torch and maneuvered your ideas of retirement to where money no longer became a necessity for survival, but rather a want for the pretentiousness of society deemed acceptable and ascertainable. The crown of glory once aspired and associated with being a super grandparent, no longer held the same ideas of matriarchal and patriarchal grandeurs, but instead interfered with the concepts of overtime, pensions, 401k's, and retirement. Life, right?

We fight with ourselves, and often at times with not only the cake, but the conveyance, deed and equitable stake in the bakery store we purchased the cake from. We can no longer see the simple joys in the simple milestones that are social occurrences, and memories in the small and invaluable moments. No man would want to hear his wife say she is leaving you for another man since she felt alone when you were trying to acquire the whole world for her; however, in the process of acquiring the world for her, you left your front door wide open and her serenity unkept, in the interim of said success and societal acquiesce.

When you acquire enough assets and materialistic objects, when do you stop for the sake of family and obtain (plus maintain) family balance? Do not be greedy or classified as "gluttonous for money", which is a compound sin leading to vanity. Again, this notion of acceptance and silent mandates of societal pressures and norms to fit in to be widely accepted among the masses are in vain. What we should be, how much we should make, when we should be it, and how we should be it are individual journeys and not subjected to mass approval. Achieve on your own time. "The masses are always wrong" in the words of a good friend of mine. In my opinion, as a frontline veteran privy with the observation and complexities of married private officers, sergeants, lieutenants and the military police, in which I was assigned to while enlisted, it is from years of observation that I personally believe that the divorce rate is so high because people eventually find out the hard way, that they married not the partner which they took vows for, but the deafening silence of the marital room, the empty bed, empty dinner tables, and the ambiguity and vagueness of the tours one's partners would partake in, at any given time those tours do not only plague the military marriages.

Through prayer, trials, tribulations, patience, understanding, and experience through traveling, wisdom was giving to me. God sent wisdom through me to build companies and countries throughout the globe. Nevertheless, it was wisdom who asked me, "Am I satisfying the needs of my family or the needs of vanity and people?" My family and friends just need me, and I just needed to be successful. I thank God for wisdom even when wisdom questions me.

Chapter 2
Who I Am "That's Elementary, My Dear"!

My ambitions to achieve success was infused in me from my mother and my early stages of childhood. As I traveled with her to her job, I would observe her in her natural atmosphere at work. How she answered the phone, how she typed, and how she spoke to her colleagues. I picked up those work habits while observing her, and it was with those work ethics that I knew those were the building blocks I needed to ensure that my children did not grow up in the same environment I did. My mother, my main influencer, worked for Child Support Enforcement, and she told me to never let my name cross her desk. I humbly followed her orders for I am the youngest of my Mother's, three children we all have biblical names (each name has a beautiful meaning – look them up). My oldest brother's name is Astyages, my sister's name is Esdras, and mine is Simeon. I was born on May 4, 1988, at 10:00pm, in Northside Hospital, located in Atlanta, Georgia. My two siblings were born at Grady Hospital. My Mother was married at the time to my Father, who has a biblical name like mine, Tobit

Sariel Nunnally. My Mother's name is Sonya and she was born on April 18, 1965, in Albuquerque, New Mexico. My Mother is the oldest of 5 siblings.

As a child, I once asked my Mother what her favorite memory from her childhood was. She told me she used to lay in the grass when she was a kid and look up at the clouds and talk to God. I smiled as she shared the intimate memory with me and thought how peaceful it all sounded. I knew no matter what I achieved in my life, I needed to make sure my kids have a plot of grass they could lie in and look up to the sky to speak to God as well. In order to achieve that goal, I would need money of course. Right?

Our family lived in a house on Tiger Flower Drive when I was born, which is the home that we returned to after coming home from the hospital's delivery unit. The earliest memory that I could muster up when living at Tiger Flower Drive, involved a toy fire truck, which I put under my pillow. I used to bump my head against this toy fire truck, until I fell asleep. It seems that the subtle process of giving myself a slight concussion was somehow therapeutic and lulling to me. I guess kids will be kids!

However, my mother and dad were not wealthy in money, but my mother was wealthy in wisdom and a work ethic that could not be matched. The memories she left me were more precious than money or gold. I can remember surprisingly and vividly the inside of the house, the nostalgic smell of fresh herbs on my Mom's windowpane, and the comforting smell of vanilla perfumed incense burning by Mom's patio door as she hummed one of her favorite songs. When coming out of my room, in which the bottom bunk bed was my domain. I remembered that my Mother's room was on the left side of my bedroom and the living room was straight ahead and down the hall. To be honest, it still fascinates me to this day that I am even able to hold on to any nostalgic memories from our home on Tiger Flower Drive, due to my youthful age. Yet, those memories would be a segue for the streams of different homes that we would find ourselves moving from time-to-time, over the years.

Family is priceless, my Mom found a new apartment home for us in Wellington Court. Later that year, we moved from Fulton County and to DeKalb County to Wellington Court Apartments, which was located in the City of Decatur. Everything I thought I knew was immediately changed as I walked into our new unit holding my favorite GI Joe Soldier toy. I, unable to grasp and understand the quiet sense of both excitement and fear in starting over, for lack of adolescent choice of words. Yet, what I wouldn't foresee standing in the foyer as our home began to fill up with cardboard boxes being taken off the moving truck my Mother's family was able to use to assist us with our move across town, was the amazing memories that Wellington Court would provide for me in my foundational and impressionable years as a young boy growing up.

I would be remiss to not admit that Wellington Court was home and proved to be a conjunction of so many of my firsts! My first water fight, my first football game, the first time I a received a punishment from my Mother, my first walk to the one cent candy store with my sister, and the first time I thought innocently that one day I would make one million dollars so that I could buy all of the candy in the one cent candy store. Such youthful ambitions, such trivial naivety. Yet, wise enough to know that by the time I obtain one million dollars, it would not be the same as the present day. I understood inflation at a young age.

I loved the Wellington Court Apartment Community, and the memories of my youth experiences are time stamped in the concrete and grass fields. I would be engrossed with the smells of my Mom's cooking while she hummed in her favorite summer dress. During the summer days, the breeze would blow her sheer curtains back and forth, spreading the aroma of her cooking throughout the house, creating a euphoric serenity needed when the summer heat made it impossible to do anything but watch my love, my Mother, from the living room couch. My mother could cook anything, however, I could still close my eyes and smile as the smell of my Mom's delicious well-seasoned baked turkey, baked macaroni and cheese, and collard greens filling my nostrils for Sunday dinner while watching the movie Soul Food. Good times. Since I was the youngest of three, I always wanted three kids in the order in which we were born. Two sons to play football with and teach business to and a daughter whom I could love on in the same fashion my mother loved me. However, I knew I would not birth any child into poverty meaning, I would need a lot of money. The thoughts of a child, innocent and pure.

My Mom was an amazing cook like stated before, and an amazing Mother. The only thing about her I would change would be her length of time she had on Earth. Some of my fondest memories include her presence and closeness to me, and her representation and provisions of love, protection, and nurture. She taught me about the power of God and shared with me her love of music. I remembered distinctly listening to the record player belt out "Oh Happy Days", by the Edwin Hawkins Singers. A song that I would literally listen to every single morning, before going to school.

As a new resident of Decatur, I would be exposed to a government program and initiative called, "Minority to Majority", also referred to as M-to-M. In other words, the State of Georgia's legislature would integrate residents from my community of Decatur in the 90's to the upper-middle class community of Tucker, Georgia, in the same year. This exchange happened through the means of school integration and inclusion; also known as "cultural cross-pollination". Of course, I was unaware of the historical significance of why I would attend an educational institution with other students who did not reside in my neighborhood. Nevertheless, I was aware of the changes I had to make to participate in this volunteer program. Interestingly enough, it was these types of scenarios that I would master with life, while life foreshadowed the upcoming experiences I would experience in the world of business and in the diplomatic space. I would have to adjust to the ever so demanding schedules of entrepreneurship. I would learn how to master demanding tasks while being deprived of sleep as a child, not in the form of abuse, of course, nevertheless, still a very valuable trait not too many people can execute.

When I was eight years old, I had to wake up at 5:00 am to catch the public school bus to Memorial Stadium. I would then wait to get on another bus that would ultimately take me to Brockett Elementary School, driven by Mrs. Judith Medes. Mrs. Judith Medes was strict, which meant being late to the bus stop was not an option. As a child, I learned how to deal with her personality, a great trait to learn in the business setting. The trek from the Wellington Court Apartment Community to the bus stop was an arduous one, but one would prove to be meaningful. The responsibility of waking up on time and getting ready for school was the responsibility of us, my siblings and I, as children. This was, and is, part of my success, determination, and discipline (using both determination and discipline to complete the tasks others do not want to).

Going to a different school outside of my community allowed me to be open to learning and understanding other cultures and communities, which helped me live and understand the phrase, "When you are in Rome, do as the Romans do", but you first need to understand how the Romans operate. After, you understand how the Romans operate, next accept the fact that no matter how much you learn from their culture, you will never be a Roman, period. No matter your race, religion, skin tone, or nationality, if you are rich or poor, if you are a believer or a non-believer, well known or just getting started, God made us all so love yourself and who God made you to be. You are God's favorite just like me.

Nevertheless, busing children from the urban-suburban communities to the upper-middle-class communities allowed the state to participate in cultural cross-pollination. When my Mother learned of the Minority-to-Majority academic initiative, she immediately signed my siblings and I up. I'm not sure what gave her the insight and foresight that the integration experience would be a life-changing one, and one that would shape me for years to come. I am grateful that her intuition and penchant for education shone through with her decision to enroll us into the program. My Mom was very dedicated to the importance of us receiving the best academic opportunities and invested in our educational paths. I am still amazed at her zeal for our education, homework, and her taking the time out to read quizzes and spelling tests. In between these tasks, she would be making dinner for us kids and packing up our school lunches the night before so that we didn't miss the bus. This is how I treat my team as well. I make sure I take the time out to mentor my team at least once a week. I give them access to me because you never know how much people value the one-on-

one time with you and you never know what they are going through as well at home.

My Mom worked three jobs, and offered her expression of love through solely providing for us children financially and cultivating learning opportunities that she knew one day would shape our futures. She was selfless and did not complain. She was beautiful and stoic, direct but kind. Hence, my leadership style. I could talk to her about anything, even as a child, and her presence was always calming and effective with me. She provided a love that was unmeasurable to me and equipped me with the foundation of my faith in God, my love for Christ, and the understanding of the Holy Spirit. We would read the bible together, which is why I read the bible with my daughter.

She was a simple woman with a vibrant and consistent spirit. She also loved her children. It is that love that would motivate me to make her proud as a young man at Brockett Elementary School through the Minority-to-Majority program. Again when I was a child, the State of Georgia implemented the M-to-M program for desegregation purposes, in doing so, they brought together many different people from different communities. I understood and learned that practice, which benefited me tremendously in the International Business World.

My experience at Brockett Elementary School afforded me an accelerated and invaluable conduit of learning how to accept and interact with different cultures, at such a young and impressionable age. Customarily, my neighborhood at Wellington Court Apartments, was predominately black. However, at Brockett Elementary school, the population and majority of the student body was Caucasian. It transported me into a world unknown and quickly forced me to learn and assimilate into an environment, so unlike what I knew. True to form, the school afforded me a novel experience, unfounded in the educational institutions in my African-American community, and encouraged unprecedented learning opportunities for us as children. One such opportunity was learning the German language in the fifth grade. Poignantly, it is my oracular exposure to the German culture and studying of its language at Brockett Elementary School that would later allow me the ability to easily assimilate into the international post that the United States Army would assign me to after enlisting, which ironically would be in the country of Germany. By then, I knew how to fit into German culture. I wish I would've known African culture as well too as a child. Could you imagine learning everything about the Continent of Africa and Europe? That would open a child's mind up completely.

One would probably assume in such a racially-driven integration experiment it would breed or beget a level of hate or racial tension felt in either the community or school hallways. However, interestingly enough we were all enamored amongst the school body. I, for one, loved my experience at Brockett Elementary School. In all reality, with my participation in the Minority-to-Majority program, the communal warmth was the same from Wellington Court to Brockett Elementary School. Which in turn made it easier for me when I am doing my favorite late-night flight from D.C. to Dubai or Dubai to Africa. I was open to trying all the different cuisines when traveling due to the fact that I was never treated any differently each day in Elementary School. My teachers genuinely embraced me and the other minority students, which ensured our seamless transition to a world so unlike our own. Seeing other individuals who resembled myself also allowed the transition to be seamless. It helped further that I was able to see other adults, staff and faculty members who also looked like me. One of those adults would be a janitor named Mr. Azariah, who would later become my mentor in the 2nd grade.

Mr. Azariah was a 6'3", African-American man who I could only describe as stoic, quiet, serious, and kind. His eyes were very intuitive, and he possessed a spirit of patience and resilience that I was unused to as a young male. To a young child being raised in Decatur, Georgia, Mr. Azariah more than just a janitor to me in an Elementary School. He was a Father Figure, a friend, and an introduction to a form of familial normalcy. I would swell up with pride when he referred to me as his 4th son, which would instill in me the confidence that every young man needs, to have an adult male to shadow, inspire to, make proud and emulate.

I often at times ponder what made Mr. Azariah choose me. What did he see in me, or what is it that he didn't see around me to make him reach out to me? What did he notice I needed, that he knew that he could fulfill? Regardless of Mr. Azariah quiet and authoritative demeanor, his compassion was the quality that truly preceded him. Due to the fact that my Mother, who found herself believing to be a Master Barber, and I, her loving son and unsuspectingly her at home barber shop guinea pig. However, no Master Barber south of the Mason-Dixie line, who saw my Mother's results, would proudly give her a standing ovation as a dominant master barber. Therefore, my haircuts by my mother were so whimsical that janitors took pity on me. Ironically, everyone says treat the janitor and the CEO in the same fashion. I guess you can say God sent a janitor to teach me how to be a CEO, and I am extremely thankful for him to this day.

Mr. Azariah didn't stop there and would prove to play an incessant and significant role in my childhood. It was Mr. Azariah that would later convince my Mother to allow me to sign up to play football for the Tucker Football League. Yet, with all things that manifest into our lives, the balance of the good is often at times in parallel with the unwanted existence of "bad". We to experience both good and bad bilaterally during the trials and exploration of our lives. At home, life prove to be a constant battleground, with the full severity of my physical battles unbeknownst to my Mother. However, it was Mr. Azariah that offset my unhappiness at home. He would prove himself to be the epitome of male provided guidance.

"Blood is Meaner Than Water"

The most interesting thing is people who love you the most sometimes love you the hardest, it is up to you to decide if that love is healthy for you or not. I would encourage healthy love. Nevertheless, everything changed overnight and shattered the naivety and innocence of my youth when my Mother made the decision to allow a troubled family member to move in with us, after he was having no place to go. With my Mother's work schedule being ever so demanding, due to working three jobs to take care of her children, her decision would prove disastrous for me and reshape my life from one of free spirit to learning how to daily maneuver past the tyrannical outbursts and attacks from a troubled teen. This gentleman taught me how to deal with insubordinates in all walks of life.

In the business world, fighting is not an option, however, the pen is mightier than the sword. He who holds the pen wins the battle. I learned how to deal with anger, and I understood what was meant by "Vengeance is mine said the Lord".

In life, you will cross those you thought were family, but they end up being the people who prove not to be family at all. "Business is war" in the words of another mentor of mine. Be advised to use wisdom in business and in life to identify who your real angels are, and the wolves in sheep's clothing. Protect your family at all cost and never forget, with Adam and Eve, the snake went to Eve. The enemy will be eager to meet your family and business partners to cause chaos. Use wisdom to identify red flags and remove these people immediately, not only in business, but in your relationships as well.

As a teen, this gentleman taught me so much about the movements of the enemy. He would prove to be my introduction to child abuse, both physically and mentally. Even in his youth, he was the true definition of a tyrant and found himself dedicated to torment. His cause, my harm, fear, and my pubescent inability to physically fight him back due to adolescent fear, and his mere strength that acquired only six years my senior. He toppled over my smaller and undeveloped frame at that time of course. His strength caused me undue anxiety during my childhood, displacement and apprehension in a home once riddled with amazing memories and genuine happiness that I innately had before the abuse. Nevertheless, I would use that energy and drive in the future and turn it into desire and ambition to complete any task I felt God sent me to accomplish. I understand that determination and hard work yields great results. I encourage you to use any energy to tap into those traits at all times.

Home became a battlefield, and I lived with the real-life version of the monster that children believe to live under beds and in closets. Regardless of the fact that this family member had a plethora of loved ones and family members who cared for him enough to open their doors to allow him a haven of support and shelter, he nonetheless rebelled consistently and always chose violence, bullying, anger, fighting and his temper to guide his decisions unfruitfully! The perfect place to practice how to overcome adversity and accomplish a task. Even the monster at home cannot stop me from accomplishing the mission outside, focus and attack your goals with vigor. I have an obsession for achieving goals and making my God happy.

Unfortunately, his obsession with sporadically pummeling me, hurling insults at me, driving his fist into my face or back of my head, did not only stop at home. He consistently found himself in the thralls and middle of every fight he could provoke or not turn away from them. A chip on his shoulder was an understatement! It was more like a boulder. It was very common to come home from school and find out from my Mom that she had to leave work early because this family member got into a fight at school and used a computer keyboard to physically attack and beat up another student at school. Fortunately for me, he only conditioned me for the personalities of the real world. I did not expect anyone to give me anything since I could not receive protection in my house. I had to learn how to protect myself, which taught me how to protect my business and my family.

I would be remiss to not admit what I discovered in time, being the issue with this family member and what his anger, temper and unwarranted violence all met. Often, as parents, we sometimes forget that short-term decisions could change the trajectory of a child's life. When his Father expelled him from his home and my Mother accepted him to our home, no one could really identify how much he longed for his Father. The rejection and displacement by his Father, although it doesn't justify the monstrosities. It allowed me to identify with his own insecurities as a young child trying to quiet the noise of being unwanted. Fortunately for me, I could not correlate the understanding of the mental distress someone would go to that felt like they were being rejected by someone they truly loved. From the standpoint of a man to a woman is one situation however, from a son to a father, I am sure that is tough, even if it is only a psychological misunderstanding and not a physical truth.

To be honest, during his time staying with us, the only person I believe made any headway with him to quell his anger and temper was one of my Mother's boyfriends named Jasher, (yes also a biblical name, Google the meaning). Jasher would understand the importance of quality time prior to it becoming a sensationalized love language. Quality time that consisted of playing video games and going on walks where he would talk with him, and spend time with him, consistently! Jasher never undermined and always looked at his heart. For this reason, my family member truly valued Jasher. Prior to Jasher's unsolicited intervention, my family member was truly a lost and daunting cause, as far as lost causes went, for I still had the scars and injuries to prove it.

Oddly in some ways, this family member was one of my biggest fans as well as my biggest abuser. The dichotomy of this would plague me for years to come prior to permanently leaving home and joining The Army. It would initiate an unsuspecting Stockholm effect during those times. Regardless, I genuinely love this family member to this day.

The physical rage and emotional abuse that I was subjected to, due to the inability to find the genuine love that he so desired. The vulnerabilities that were birthed from his parents getting a divorce, encouraged him to dull the pain of these life-changes he couldn't control by using his anger. Typical adolescents, the thought they can control everything with anger. Irrespective of knowing that he was just an insecure child and hurt person within, what the world saw was a confident young black male who although seemed to get into trouble here and there and into a fight or two whenever he could manage, he was also a talented athlete. This would feed his ego, enable his bad conduct and helped breed a vain persona that temporarily and superficially depends on what he achieved on the gridiron and courts for our schools, on Friday night and Saturday morning games!

An impeccable and stellar athlete, and he truly and easily mastered the sport of football and probably could master all sports. Football gave him purpose and passion after the divorce and finally found his footing and place in society, the community, and our home. Yet again, this is what you create when you remove a dad from the house and destroy the family unit. The men will search for their identity during the impressionable years. And the young girl will search for their confidence and miss their genuine love from their dad. They will miss that whisper in their ear "Good morning, baby girl, rise and shine my love". These are the principals that families are based on. Business interferes with these values from time to time.

My sister on the other had so much promise and potential in life. She was amazing. With a Mom like ours who was constantly at work providing for her family, my sister became what I guess some would call a second Mom. We went everywhere together when we were younger. She was my first best friend and I loved her ardently. Through her love for education, she inspired my love for education, and would also educate me tremendously about women and give me an insight into a female's brain and their way of thinking. This would be priceless to me later as not only a man who would have meaningful relationships with women, but as a young man who would one day give birth to a beautiful, loving daughter.

My sister, Esdras, (also a biblical name the meaning of her name is beautiful as well) was beautiful and truly a breath of fresh air and offset the physical abuse, that she too had to endure. Her taking up for me, or trying to protect me from the attacks, would often at times lead to her own demise and pummeling, which gave me closure when her interventions became less and less to ensure her own childlike and instinctive survival. Perfect as she taught me how to defend my loved ones too. I defended my soldiers in the Army and defended my employees in the business world due to the fact that we were living with the constant and sporadic fears of being beaten without warrant or provocation. We made good of our childhood summer days and still did things that other kids did, protect your loved ones.

We had water fights together with the other kids at our

Wellington Court Apartment complex in Decatur, Georgia. Back in the 90's, when I was about nine years old, and everyone was ready to go to FreakNik. We were on the balcony and kids in our neighborhood were walking underneath our balcony and patio, and my sister would call their names causing them to look up and then… splash!! She would dump huge pots of water on them initiating huge neighborhood water fights. All the kids would emphatically come outside with water balloons, water guns, and pots of water, and we would have an absolute ball! After the water fight, we would play football, and the girls would cheer us on until the streetlights came on and it was time to go inside. Oh, such good times in Decatur, Georgia. I use these events in the business world to keep the energy good at the Office. Not just potlucks, but bowling games for lunch, golf for lunch, enjoyable activities to balance out stressful environments.

I missed the days when the rigors and responsibilities of adulthood hadn't begun, and where the innocence and sincerity of my childhood was my compass. I remember the days in which I would lay still in the grass like my mom used to and smell the honeysuckle on the neighborhood trees, and watch the glistening of the sun peak through the trees, as I stretched my hand in attempt to grab a sun ray and timestamp the moment of reverence for God. Laying there, I could hear the sounds and life of the community moving all around me. I could hear pots and pans clanking as someone's grandmother cooked for the family and most likely the neighborhood kids who would straggle in with a friend to quiet the loneliness of their own home, and home cooked meals that they knew wouldn't be waiting for them in a dark house where parents would be at work. Yet, we were a community. We were lock-key kids, and we were just members of a village in which we had no say or control. We were children.

For me, one of the magical things about nighttime in Decatur, a clear moon in a perfect sky …would be my wonder of lightening bugs. The sporadic, or systemic, glow of the lightening bug truly enraptured me, and reminded me how truly poetic and artistic that God was as the Creator of all things. It humbled me as a child and something as little as seeing a bug glow no differently than a hallway light in my Mom's home enthralled me as a child, and my love for nature and science at such a young age. The lightening bugs would pass me, and I would attempt to catch one in both hands. Only to peak in with one eye to see him light up in my hand, and then I would let him go. Yet, the peacefulness of childhood doesn't always last, and peace can always be shattered by the unexpectedness of life. I guess, in the end, everything needs a balance. Balance your books at the office, balance your taxes, balance time with your family, balance time with your kids, and most importantly balance time with your God.

My sister Esdras called me into her room one day. She was crying hysterically and sobbing, and my stomach immediately dropped in fear, as I asked her what was wrong. It seems that she got bad grades in school. Me being a naïve 11-year-old little brother who imagined himself to be a protective man for her in that moment, I promised her that everything was going to be okay. The next morning, my Sister was gone! When I asked my Mother where Esdras was, she told me she sent her to my Aunt's house to live in order for her to raise her grades. I was crushed! Expect the unexpected, but always focus on the best.

Since I was a young child, my sister Esdras was my best friend. In one moment, my world came crashing down because at the age of fifteen, she was being sent away for bad grades in school. My Mom was still working three jobs. My tyrannical abuser was only a door away from my bedroom. Esdras could no longer defend me from his blows. I had no one to laugh with, dream with, and talk to anymore. She was my confidant, a helper, and, a nurturer to me. She was the funniest woman I knew, my Esdras was my second example and testament of genuine, unconditional love and friendship. As a young male, maneuvering through life in the Wellington Court's Community, my sister's room sitting eerily vacant and dark unsettled and disturbed me. It also popped the peace bubble we were able to create in a world of unexpected trials and familial independence. I had no idea when my Sister would be coming back, and my ideas of peace and serenity at home was destroyed and no longer attainable. This reminds me of when I had a huge business deal and one day the other team just pulled out without a reason. I was blown, however, God blessed me with something better. When one door closes for ways that don't make sense to you, and you put forth all efforts for amicable resolutions, then it is for a good reason just keep walking, trust the process, and stay focused.

I'm not sure if I slept the first couple of days she was sent away, and more painful than her absence and my fatigue was the inability to hear her voice during those first few days. Regardless of how strong she was, and the fact she practiced tough love here and there, she was, nevertheless, the only sister I'd known since we were kids. The first phone call I finally received from her, since she was sent away, happened on the day I had one of my football games. As someone who was always one of my constant supporters as an athlete, her call was to wish me good luck and to encourage me on the gridiron.

When it came to football, I was truly passionate about the sport and very talented in the craft. I was grateful that my mentor Mr. Azariah convinced my mother to let me join the team. My family knew I was going to the NFL, and that my talent for the sport could be a conduit for school and a professional career. The day that my sister would call me from my aunt's house to wish me luck truly had an impact because we won the games! I scored three touchdowns in the first game, and another three in the second game. It was a jamboree!

Due to my sheer will and natural speed, I was fast enough to play offense. The coach put me in as a running back and wide receiver. On the defense side of things, I was also fast enough to play safety, corner, and outside linebacker. I was also sharp and agile enough to play defensive lineman and add that to agility. I was beating people off the line causing fumbles and sacks every game just like in the first jamboree that we won. I loved football back then. Of all the positions, I played my favorite was running back. We won games that season and I was slotted to the All-Stars final game, in which we also won and took home the trophy!

The next season, however, was different. My coach asked me what position I wanted to play. Yet, I was so quiet that he picked for me. He chose Wide Receiver, which was my least favorite position, but nonetheless, I went along with it. Back then, I was unable to stand up and speak for myself because, abuse at the house ended up removing the self-confidence I had. With every strike of his fist, slam to the ground, and painful kick from his foot. In the end, with Esdras gone and my Mother at one of her jobs, I quickly learned that the football field was my only way away from him. It seemed that because of this conundrum of loneliness, pain, and familial apprehension I naturally began acting out at school. Irrespective of my love for education, being smart and my now average grades, issues at home overwhelmed me. Like mentioned before, in fifth grade I learned how to speak the German language. Although, the teachers didn't understand the contradiction of me. How could I be so polite and do well in all my classes, but then act out insubordinately in other ways? This helps me better identify issues with colleagues and respond to them better with an open mind. First trying to resolve issues because we as people never are fully aware of what the other person is going through. It's up to us to be compassionate.

As a minority student, being bused in from Decatur to Tucker in the 90's, it was really the Europeans teachers first experience being exposed to such an array of minority students who like me was dealing with such tough challenges behind closed doors, such as being physically assaulted at home. What are the tale tell signs of juvenile abuse at home? Who at school could I tell that my family member slammed my head against the floor so hard, one time, after he watched a WCW episode, and now he think he is the 15 year old version of Diamond Dallas Page, that my right ear drums began to bleed for the rest of the night. Who would understand that I would make sure to wipe all traces of the blood and my injury away before my mom came home, in fear of his retaliation and retribution if I told on him again.

Obviously, these mandated state reporters weren't yet equipped enough to identify the abuse and my behavior wasn't enough to alarm them to investigate my home life. No one understood my cuts, bruising on darker skins, and constant scars were from the physical abuse I endured at home and not football. Can you identify if anyone in your house or business is going through anything? Sometimes a prayer is all they need but a helping hand is always invaluable.

One day, that same family member would slam my head against the metal part of the bunk bed, splitting open the back of my skull. The injury would require stitches. When I went to the hospital, yet days after the injury I woke up like normal and immediately fell to the ground as soon as I attempted to stand up from out of the bed. I immediately knew that something was wrong and in a quiet panic, I tried to stand up again and saw that I was unable to walk and that my legs were like Jello. Due to the fact I had the strong urge to use the bathroom and unwilling to use the bathroom on myself, I crawled across my room floor using my arms with rhythmic determination. Right arm first, followed by my left arm. Right arm, left arm, right arm, left arm. A method that I would later learn in the Army was low crawling.

Finally making it to the bathroom, I was able to hoist myself up using the frame of the toilet as an anchor. I had some strength in my knees, so my knees were able to hold me up high enough to successfully use the toilet. After relieving myself, I crawled back to my room. However, on my way back to my bedroom, fate intervened, and my Mother opened the door to her master bedroom to find me crawling down the hallway and dragging myself along. My Mother…my first love, my first concept of a wife. She immediately dropped to the floor in a panic and asked me what was wrong?

When I told her about my inability to walk and use my legs, she immediately cancelled any plans and thoughts of going to work and rushed me to the hospital. After testing and scans, the emergency room doctor determined that my inability to walk was a direct result to the head trauma I received from when my family member cracked my head on the frame of my bunkbed. This caused these ensuing issues and subsequently required physical therapy to learn how to walk again, and master mobility. In which, one would assume, take the actuality of the bullying and juvenile intimidation and rivalry endured more seriously to something of concern.

Again, one would think! My determination is only matched by my mother. Transferring the determination into business is a huge blessing. If I had to learn how to walk again, my only fear is God. I believe I can achieve any obstacle (as anyone should). Even though, I have no desire to start over, I have the innate desire to acquire what I want to experience through many different things in life, and many different avenues and opportunities that are applicable with my talents, which allows me to gain a new perspective. These paradigms are transformations to new beginnings, and not start overs. I had to physically pick myself up and learn how to keep going, imagine the self-boost that does to you mentally. God blessed me, I can pick any company or country up and move them forward. I am business development. You should feel the same way about yourself.

Upon learning how to walk again, I returned to school with new stitches and entered my classroom smiling, as always. Oddly enough, without any intervention at home or from anyone in school, I naturally began to assume that all households were just like mine and all younger kids were subjected to physical abuse. I got accustomed to my circumstances. I truly did want a relationship with him outside of him taking his frustrations and unwavering torment out on me. Yet the friendship that I so ardently longed for, would never be. I quickly did away with childish dreams and knew that any viable relationships, and/or friendships between us, would be made outside of the home.

I ended up having two friends during elementary school. They were twins, whose names were also biblical with beautiful meanings, their names were Enoch and Baruch (Google the names). They were from Eastwyck Apartment homes in Decatur Georgia. It was right up the street from my apartment complex, Wellington Court. The twins weren't identical, they were fraternal twins born less than three minutes apart. The oldest was taller than the younger. The Twins also had a cousin in school, whose name was Jeremiah. We all became really good friends. In retrospect, we became a village of sorts. They let me into their "family at school" and "after school". We rode the bus together, and they became my brothers. At school, I would write on a piece of paper and fold it into a sort of impromptu origami, then I would slip the test answers to them to help them out.

The only time us "brothers" found ourselves competing against one another, due to sheer speed and agility in football, was on the gridiron! The twins and their cousin were truly the only challenge, and only real competition I faced as an athlete. Thoughts of childhood's youthful exuberances and tenacities as children. Prior to social media tactics, popularity was based off the premises of who was the fastest at the playground. Popularity was based off of fun! Fun was always outside feeling the energy from the sun on your skin, and the sunlight beaming on the back of your neck and ears as you laugh genuinely, ultimately getting lost in time. Oblivious to the fact you are overheating and sweating, but thankful for the breeze that God sent in to give you a brief moment of relief. School activities such as "Field Day" provided great opportunities for Baruch, Jeremiah and I, to demonstrate our innate talents, gifts, speed, and great athleticism in front of the student body.

On "Field Day", the teachers put all of us "Brothers" on the same team, and we completely annihilated any concept of competition or opposition from the rival teams. During the track and field portion of Field Day, I specifically remember during the baton relay race, the "brothers" and I, easily finished the race while the other kids were still running. I was chosen to be the last leg of our relay team and Enoch was strategically chosen as the first leg on our team. Enoch started us off with a flash of speed, and I met the precedent he set by finishing the race in the same flash of speed across the finish line to victory! To say "it was so much fun" was an understatement, and I still remember the thrill and excitement of that field day, along with the cheering from the faculty members. Mr. Azariah proudly and knowingly smiled on the sidelines as the smells of the freshly baked cookies and lemonade provided by the PTA allured us kids at the end of the games. We got to be kids that day! No worries of home life, sadness, pain, anxiety, fear, or rejection. That day was special and represented the notions of true normalcy and the youthful exuberance of childhood.

Up next, after winning the relay race, the Twins and I were geared to partake in the piggyback ride competition. Baruch and I naturally were paired up with one another. This should be a piece of cake, I thought! When our Language Arts teacher yelled on the microphone, "on your mark," I quickly hopped on Baruch back … "get set…gooooo!" We were off and we took lead easily. 100 meters, 200 meters, I looked back, and the other kids were still behind us. "We could have walked across this finish line." I smugly thought. We were home free and just like the baton relay race we will win another race! "Field day is too easy!" I said to myself and repeated out loud to Baruch. "No one is as fast as us." replied Baruch. It was a perfect day, the sun was hugging my face, not a single cloud in the sky, and no real opponent in front us. We set to presumably win another blue ribbon. Yet with hubris…comes humility.

As Baruch and I were still heavily in the lead of our peers, our team members cheered us along the piggyback relay obstacle course. Baruch misjudged the level on the ground during his next step. This miscalculation caused him to slip due to the additional weight of my being on his back added to his equally small frame. All these circumstances caused his equilibrium to be thrown off. Resulting in us both falling to the ground. While releasing my arms from around his neck, I instinctively used my left arm to brace for the fall and undeniable impact. Crack! As a kid, I also misjudged where I was going to land as the kinetic energy and adrenaline surging through my body, propelled me further than the anticipated place I assumed I was going to land. Unavoidably and unknowingly at the time that the misjudgment on my end caused me to fracture my left elbow.

Our teachers ran over to me franticly asking me, if I was, ok? However, in my mind I was a recent survivor of cranial stitches in my head and learning how to walk again. In comparison, this did not surpass my trauma scale threshold in which I quickly expanded. I ensured them bravely, that I was okay! I completed the day at school and rode the bus back home. I held my elbow the whole ride back home. Now, wreathing in pain I ventured to my definition of nourishment, my mother.

I showed her my arm, again with her parental instincts and quick decisive thinking, she loaded me into her car as we yet again headed to

Northside Hospital. Upon arrival at the hospital we went directly to the x-ray technicians in the pediatric wing. At that moment I was informed I fracture my elbow. My mother was livid, and I was too at first. Nevertheless they put my arm in a cast, being from Atlanta Georgia and being raised in Decatur, the cast represented a badge of honor for me. The whole ordeal was now more fun for me (boys will be boys). Interesting enough my mother was showering me with affections telling me everything was going to be ok. However, in my head my only thoughts were to have my cast sign as soon as I went back to school. Ahhhhh, the simple joys of a young child, who is going to sign my cast first!

Chapter 3
 Who I Am …. "Stuck in the Middle"

My Mother knew the ins and outs of all her children's personalities, nuances, quirks, and needs. She truly mastered how she would converse and handle each one of her kids. Which in the end, it took time for us to fully comprehend she was actually passing away or fully transitioning. My brother, my sister, and I chose naivety to cope with my mother's sickness. Her laughter during her battle with the most destructive terminal illness in America, kept us in a state of aloof. Breast cancer did not take her life, yet it caused her an unimaginable amount of pain. Morphine was the real villain. The body cannot fight both, Morphine and Breast Cancer.

My mother was herself until the last week of her being alive. In fact, one month before she departed from us, she surprised me by driving all the way to my place in North Atlanta to bring me donuts. Regardless of the extreme amount of pain, in which she was always in, while battling stage four breast cancer. After my mother's show of strength, who was I to take off work after her passing? When she was a single parent, she made every effort to always spend quality time with me regardless of her fatigue. The sacrifices of unconditional love of a mother are truly incomparable.

Moving around so much as a child truly prepared me for a life of traveling. Thus far I have traveled to three of the seven continents without any fear and without any urges to visit Antarctica. The ability to travel at a young age also helped me in my international travels, but we all have to start small. After leaving Brockett Elementary school, I went to Henderson Middle School. My sister was a couple of grades ahead of me and my infamous family member attended a High school in DeKalb County, Georgia. My family member also played football for the same school, and he was extremely good and very talented. One of the times I went to his game, he almost ran back a punt return on the Special Teams. The last man to tackle my family member actually grabbed his face mask to strategically tackle him by turning his neck around, to force him down. An illegal tackle of course. True to form, my family member's temper, which was always so close below the surface was immediately enraged, and he ran to the guy, took off his helmet and beat the man with his own helmet. I cannot say I was surprised, but I'm sure the school was slightly taken aback. Yet, also true to form he didn't get into trouble for the helmet attack, nor were there any consequences to his explosive behavior and blatant temper. With such starlike immunity, my family member enjoyed playing football at this school in DeKalb County, Georgia. He wasn't getting arrested for fighting or in trouble for committing random crimes here and there, he was considered to be a hero, star and football icon for the school. He had access to an unlimited opportunity to shine and hurt others, so he was clearly "right at home".

Esdras or the prodigal sibling who was allowed to return back home, was a cheerleader in Henderson Middle School and also ran track and field. She was very good and very fast and won a lot of races. Unfortunately, one day during P.E., her friend tripped her while she was running, causing her to fall and injure herself. The fall would prove to be detrimental as it would end her short-lived track and field career. Her scar is still visible on her right knee till this day. Yet, after her hiatus and exile of sorts, she was just happy to be back amongst her friends and peers in a neighborhood that was hers and learned complacency in the simplest of things. After she fell in track she never ran again. Did you see the difference? My love Esdra did not run track again after her fall, I had to learn how to walk again after mine. Determination, drive, and perseverance will take you far! If you ever fall in business or in a relationship, or with God or in life, get up and keep going! Your kids, your family, and your own confidence is watching you. Conqueror your obstacles and your trials, also learn the wisdom in the trial and apply it to life and business. You better not go viral being a quitter, you better go viral being a conqueror!

My mother worked three jobs while we were growing up. Due to her work load I enjoyed making her laugh every chance that presented itself. Every day before school when I was a child, I would call my mother on her work line when I rose from sleep. "Child Support Enforcement this is Sonya speaking how can I help you?" She would answer. "Are you working hard?" I would ask her. She knew it was me, so she would cheerfully reply, "Yes Simeon I am working hard." Then I would follow up with "Are you working hard for the money like in the song and she would say?" "Yes, Simeon" she would say while smiling through the phone. I dedicated myself to making my mother laugh. It would later become an inside joke between us, for years to come.

We ended up moving to Treehills Apartments on South Hairston Road. This move cause me to involuntarily leave my current school and friends and reluctantly enrolling and transferring to Miller Grove Middle School. My mother purchased my infamous family member a jeep truck and he used to blast his favorite R. Kelly song "Seems like you're ready" every day, while being charged by my mother with driving me to Miller Grove Junior High School. At home his tyrannical reign was still in existence, and he continued finding pleasure in his unprovoked and violence which led to incessant fights between us as I conditioned myself to fight back more and more each time. These fights would happen all the time my mother was at work. Each time Esdras would hide in the oblivious world of being a teenager and hanging with her two closest friends at the time, Naomi and Anna. Needless to say, with the battles for survival and serenity I was tasked with each day, I barely passed the 7th grade and my Mother was less than excited and thrilled about that! As a result, she made the decision to hold me back to repeat the 7th grade and made yet another decision to move us to Gwinnett County, where I ended up attending Shiloh Middle School as a 7th grader… once again and still did not quit in fact.

While at Shiloh Middle School, I started expressing myself more, thus finding my passion for writing. My teachers in school, were Mrs. Leah, Mrs. Delilah and Mrs. Abigail. Gwinnett County was peaceful until September 11th. I remember distinctly, as if it was only yesterday, that I was in Mrs. Leah class when the first plane struck the World Trade Center followed by the second plane. The school was told that all students were to report to our assigned homerooms, as we continued to watch in collective and communal horrors as the events continued to unfold throughout the day. We were not allowed to leave the school.

The ironic thing about sitting there watching on television the Twin Towers fall, both once known stoic pillars and trademarks that represented the strength and wealth of our country, was the almost prophetic foresight that I would one day enlist in the Army at the age of seventeen and join the same war in Iraq that would defend my country, from such further attacks. Who would have also imagined I would also one day be elected as the Vice-President of Business Development for the World Trade Center, here in Atlanta, Georgia, and I was currently watching my future headquarters fall. Mere coincidence … or divinatory destiny?

At Shiloh Middle School, I had two really good friends who also were like brothers to me. One of those friends' names was Asher and the other one named Caleb, both biblical names. Asher was from Chicago and Caleb was from St. Petersburg Florida. Caleb and I stayed in the same neighborhood, so we rode the bus together every day. We'd talk to one girl, and the other would talk to her friend. His Mom knew my Mom, and we hung out at each other's houses all the time. I stayed in the back of the neighborhood whereby, his place was more upfront of my apartments, in Gwinnett County. I remember Caleb, having a huge crush on this girl named Abel. I chuckled as I used to see it in his eyes every day. We would go to school, and he would hit me on the arm and his whole face would begin to glow with the biggest smile and then he would ask me, "Man, you see Abel today?" That was truly the highlight of his whole day. Expectedly, his infatuation and admiration of her came with consequences. One time, he got into a physical fight and altercation with Abel's actual boyfriend, so I assume he didn't appreciate Caleb stares and his compliments to Abel.

To this day, Caleb is still like a brother to me. Unfortunately, his Mother passed away when we were kids and he had to move back to Florida, thus leaving me and Asher at School. Nonetheless, Asher and I made do, and we were truly inseparable back then. We used to walk to school when the weather was good, just to be different and not conform to taking the bus like "those other kids". I used to spend the night at his house when my Mother worked late just so I could have peace and avoid unsolicited battles, by simply avoiding being at the house. I remember sitting outside Asher house at nighttime just looking up at the moon and the stars to embrace the euphoria, calm and the essence of the night air and allowing it to fully surround and immerse me in an energy and coolness I could feel amongst my skin. So refreshing, so safe! Just the thought of being briefly free from my family member's juvenile and delinquent blows and hits, and free from the mental and physical restrictions of all the fighting, in that moment looking up at the night sky was enough to repress and provisionally erase the turmoil I have managed to survive. Asher's friendship and family's acceptance of me was a haven, school and the explorative years of my life proved to also be a safe space and refuge.

My ability to write started show casing in middle school, the writing talent is extremely vital in business. If you cannot write you remove one of your ways to communicate with people. If you cannot communicate with people, you are even more futile in business. One day in language arts class, my teacher Mrs. Delilah, asked us to write a poem. She instructed that she wasn't requiring anything over the top or fantastic, but just wanted us to write a basic poem as a classroom exercise and assignment. I wrote a poem as instructed, but I didn't really think too much about it. I turned in my classroom exercise and went home for the day. The next day I returned to school and as soon as I walked into Mrs. Delilah's class. She stopped me immediately pulled me aside and asked me did I copy the poem I wrote from some other source. I told her no, I didn't and only wrote a poem after she explained the assignment to our class yesterday. She said okay and proceeded in giving me glowing reviews. I was excited! I found a new niche and talent. She told me about a contest that was up coming and the opportunity for my poems to be in the "Shiloh Silhouette" which was the school's publication of literary work gathered together from talented members of the student body. I was happy of course it was the first time I actually had someone outside my Mother, Esdras, and Mr. Azariah who actually believe in me. They believed that I could do any impressive thing if I decided to focus on it. My mother and my family knew I was talented at football but, outside of sports, my circle was small and impenetrable.

Mrs. Delilah expected me to write something good, as far as classroom bragging rights went in the faculty break room. I was to be her secret weapon and she knew that her secret was safe with me. I knew I had to write something good for the Silhouette and I did not want to let her down.

The night before writing a poem, I went to my Sister's room attempting to gather some form of inspiration. Her and her friends was partying and celebrating since she recently just got accepted into Georgia Southern University. While attempting to Google ideas for the poem, I heard my sister talking to her friend regarding her relationship status. Pointless and irrelevant talk to my young ears, but I did listen and pay heed to her describing her ideas of a knight in shining armor. Ironically, my Mother was also reading a book called, "A Knight in Shining Armor", and right then and there I thought to myself, I think I have my topic.

The next day I entered the classroom and Mrs. Delilah asked us to write a poem. She explained that all the best work will be reviewed and assessed. All work admired and chosen by the faculty, would then be published in the school's very own, "Shiloh Silhouette". I was very excited! I had a lot to write, ideas flooded my head! I started my poem off saying "Last night I was sleeping and I dreamt of you and I together, men surround us and kidnapped you but I could not be without you forever. So, I gathered my armor and sword I knew every swift of my blade had to be precise, if there was ever going to be another night with you in my life …" I managed to easily write a four-page poem about retrieving my lady from two henchmen and a boss and I ultimately named the poem "Sword Dance". The school said it is the first and only time they will publish a poem in the silhouette that contained violence in it. My apologies still to this day for the violent nature of the poem, but to me I only saw a love story.

Middle School was ok with me. My Mom and I would read the bible every day after school. Even though I rather played football outside with my friends, those special memories of reading the bible with my mother will still stay with me. My mother instilled in me her love for God forever. Now, my God will stay with me in my heart, my mind, my body, and my spirit forever. Even now as a grown man and Father, I read the Bible with my daughter to ensure and solidify the spiritual bond and life lessons in which one day will guide and comfort her. I will always be thankful to my Mother for imploring me to learn about God in those foundational and formative years as a young man.

Yet, although my Mom endeavored to clothe me in faith and knowledge, she simply refused to clothe me in real life. When in eighth grade, she announced that she wasn't going to buy me clothes anymore. That was one of the greatest lessons I ever learned. She explained the importance of being responsible, and that as a young man meant that you must work hard for everything and that nothing in life would be given to you, without merit. It is this involuntary emancipation that led to my passion for business, success, and serial entrepreneurship that would be born from my early understanding of perseverance, dedication, hard work and grit.

Chapter 4
Battles create warriors "A Higher Learning ….
Called School"

My decision to go the military was one of the best choices and steppingstones that God blessed me with. My ability to adapt to changing situation continue to showcase. In Tenth Grade I transferred schools from Druid Hill High School yet again and attended Redan High School, but on the Miller Grove side since it was still being constructed. This is important as people often have trouble adapting to new environment they have a tendency to miss your old environment. However, be advised the only thing in life that is consistent is change. Always be prepared to evolve. DeKalb County approved the new building of a new School called Miller Grove High School. My neighborhood was zoned to attend the school. We attended Miller Grove High School but, we were also separated from the kids who was permanently attending Redan. Tenth Grade was a fight in itself however, I learned not to quit. Even when giving the opportunity too never quit. Endure your challenges and do not let it change anything about you accept the amount of motivation you have to accomplish your goal.

A quick story about perseverance and overcoming obstacles as a child, we all had the lovers quarrel as kids. I was good friends with this guy in my neighborhood, his name was Noah. He got along with everyone for the most part. In school, there was a girl that really liked me. This young gentleman named Ethan wasn't happy about that. He approached me about it and what could have been a simple conversation and nothing major, escalated to unnecessary new heights. Instead of talking to me about any issues that he had, Ethan involved his older cousin in his campaign.

Ethan's cousin was Noah who lived in my neighborhood. While at my neighbor's house one day, who was visiting from New York, Noah came to my house and said, "You have any problems with my cousin?". "Not, that I knew of, but I would encourage you not to get loose on this side of the neighborhood with those words." I said. The next day we were on the bus, and Noah approached me again this time with one of his friends. I explained to them not to try to intimidate me and to keep their distance, and they agreed and walked off. I went to class.

Ethan again came up to me while at school and announced that his cousin was going to come to my house after school was over. I went home and sure enough his cousin came to my house. This time he was brandishing a weapon in which he clutched in his hand. At this time Esdras, recently given birth to a beautiful and intelligent baby girl, whom was only about six months old, and sleeping peacefully within 100 meters from where I was being threatened with a gun. To say I was livid was an understatement, I called all my family and friends to vent. I was truly upset I notified my mother about the situation. The next day I rode the bus to school the same kid came up to me yet again and asked me if I had any more issues. At that point, I had already reached my breaking point and an immediate physical altercation occurred. The Principal, whose name was Dr. Zebadiah, had to intervene in the breaking up of the fight and suspended both of us. On the way home I stopped by a friend's house named Marvin. I knocked on the door and entered. "Yoooo", I said. "My guy!" said Marvin. "What's going on?" Marvin asked. "Nothing much headed to the house." I explained. Just then, it was a knock at the door. "Come in!" exclaimed Marvin. It was Noah.

"What you are following me or something?" I asked going into a defense mode. Marvin intervened, "Is everything ok?" Marvin asked, "We just went blow for blow" said Noah. "You and Simeon?" exclaimed Marvin. "Yeah" said Noah. Marvin continued "Simeon, Noah is family, you two shake hands, end the feud, and walk out my house together. The next time I see you it should be in my house together." We agreed, we shook hands and walked out together. We left Marvin's home and I picked up a Swiss army knife that I found on the ground while walking to my home. Learning how to protect myself with a knife for fun while walking, a police officer stopped me and Noah and asked why we were not at school. We told him we were suspended, and he took me back to the school campus, as a clear indication that he had already decided that I must be lying. Upon getting out of the police car, the knife I just found fell out my pocket. In that moment, I kept walking behind the officer. The police officer walked me immediately into the school. Another officer came in with a knife she found on the ground. She immediately asked whose knife was it. Thankfully, because of my grades they ruled me out it was impossible to peg me as just a typical thug, delinquent or career problem child. They saw another man close to me and said that the knife must have fell from him and belonged to him. I couldn't allow someone to take the fall for something that they didn't do, because the knife was in fact on my person and something that I found. With the admission that the knife was indeed mine, I was found to have attempted to bring a knife onto school premises, was detained, and permanently expelled from the High School.

The knife incident resulted in me being unable to return to my High School and having to instead attend what the state called an "Alternative School" for troubled teens. Yet, I wasn't a troubled teen or any kind of delinquent. I was the example of recent incidents and years of being bullied, threatened, and physically provoked by my own home. More importantly, the officers taking me back to school; because they failed to believe that I truly was suspended from school when they questioned me while walking, is what caused me to even unwantedly be on school premises with a so called "weapon". Watching another's untruths, misunderstanding and narratives depict, redirect my life, and wrongfully label me as something that I wasn't, although unfortunate, proved to be a fruitful experience for me in a new and unexpected environment.

Being at the "Alternative School" resulted in a pretty good head space. I would have to walk a total of five daunting miles each day, when the weather permitted me to attend, as being absent wasn't an option. Ironically, it would be those same daily miles and arduous trekking that would prepare me with an endurance befitting as a member of the Army. However, when the weather didn't permit me to walk those miles, I would resort into taking the Marta Bus (public bus).

Fortunately, I was at the top of the class at my "Alternative School" and my grades were superb. The administration loved me and asked me what my plans were after leaving their school. I was actually enjoying the school; it was so different. I felt that I finally belonged and found my niche. I can focus and learn in the middle of a challenging environment. I can critically think, focus, and pay attention to my surroundings at all times. I can critically think on the fly, even in the midst of a challenging and changing environment, very valuable tools needed in life and in business. Thinking back a lot of the students who were at the "Alternative School" were considered "bad", but they were really misunderstood individuals characterized as unruly because no one had the patience to learn the backstory and the wiring that led to where they were today. In fact, it was quite the opposite and these kids at the alternative school were less unruly and just incarnate results of being part of disenfranchised neighborhoods and familial structures. I saw many naturally born and determined leaders, who possibly made some bad choices along the way out of the mere need to protect themselves during a battle that would thus negatively impact their lives and remove them from the normal stream and precedent of learning and receiving a 'regular education'. I see the good, even in the bad.

A bad choice shouldn't negatively impede the learning process of a child. It's hard enough for a child to focus on learning when they also have to focus on protecting themselves. In "Alternative School", ironically the need to defend oneself was non-existent and any such threats were eliminated through metal detectors and the unusual amount of campus security dedicated to the safety and protection of students, faculty, and staff. The school provided the protection needed for the students to excel under the provisions of PEACE and serenity. I was one of those students, a gem amongst other gems the population considered rubble.

After successfully completing Alternative School, I was sent to Shiloh High School where I would enroll into AP Chemistry courses and where I would proudly pass the Georgia High School Graduation Test with flying colors. After I directly transferred over from receiving an Alternative School education. Yet, the peace and serenity accustomed to when in alternative school was short-lived and my 11th grade year proved quite disturbing, as I had to constantly stand up for the younger Freshmen kids who were continuously being targeted, beaten, and jumped by the High School Seniors. It reminded me of how my family member would constantly attack me and physically injure me. I didn't want these Freshman to experience that same pain and trauma, that haunted me for most of my childhood with no help or reprieve in sight.

At this time, I was fully aware of how not having to worry about protection or one fending for themselves can create peace of mind in the learning world and allow one to excel.

Nevertheless, although I enjoyed my experience in "Alternative School", I did not endeavor to return there. Therefore, I learned to stay away from any bouts of trouble at Shiloh High School and instead focused all my attention solely on my studies and classwork for the first time.

It was in High School that I came into my own and started talking a lot more. Developing my ability to public speak which is important in diplomacy and giving interviews in front of large audience like I do now. The fact that I wasn't a huge fan of partying definitely helped me stay focus as well. I would routinely go to class, and then go straight home when school was out. School was a breeze for me yet, I still relied more on memory than actually studying the assigned material. My mother dropped me off to school and picked me up in our understood routine.

One day, my Mom unexpectedly quit her job. She told me that God told her to do so and to spend more time with me. I did not let her down at all and wanted to make sure that her sacrifices and adjustments were not in vain. I ended up passing Physics with a 90 and transferred to Miller Grove High School in my Senior year where I graduated from Miller Grove High School class of 07, the first graduating class. This happened after its inception under the leadership of then Principal,

Dr. Zebadiah the same Principal that would suspend me for fighting in school and later expel me for "allegedly" bringing a knife on school premises. Yet, in a divine turn of events, here I stood humble and proud on the graduation stage as an overcomer testament to perseverance and dedication. As soon as Dr. Zebadiah put my Diploma into my hand… I knew that there was no turning back. I adapted and overcame. I was ready to go into the world and to take it by storm!

Chapter 5
And Warriors Conquer

After successfully graduating from Miller Grove High School against all odds, I enrolled in Georgia Perimeter College for half a semester before deciding to join the United States Army Reserve at first and later switching over to Army Active Duty, which I learned how to work with communities from different backgrounds. Ironically, my Mother's penchant for moving us every few years into a new neighborhood, and school, would prepare me for the flexibility and accelerated assimilation skills required to adapt quickly in the Army. These arduous tasks were doable and attainable for me. I have a strong mindset, the foundation of God at my core and I believe in what the Army stands for. Duty to my family and Nation…….and free education.

Before joining the Army, each prospective and newly enlisted soldier was tasked with first successfully completing Basic Training and passing all necessary assessments and phases. I believed the best way to challenge and condition myself would be for me to actually attend Basic Training during the winter, versus doing so during the warmer weather seasons. In my mind, I figured that if I could successfully overcome my hatred for being outside and dealing with the elements of the cold by passing all Basic Training obstacles and phases during the wintertime … then in turn I could do anything! Faith, like a mustard seed, which is needed in business and every area of your life.

Reporting to Basic Training meant that I would have to make my way down to South Carolina. I was assigned to Drill Sergeant Reuben, Drill Sergeant Gideon, and Drill Sergeant Junia. As I grabbed my duffle bag from the overhead and walked toward the bus exit. I remember distinctively getting off the bus, hearing the hinges squeak and creak as the bus door closed behind me. The bus left me in a cloud of dust and the smells of the bus's exhaust, as the bus slowly sauntered down the dusty road.

Never leaving the borders of Georgia since I was a child, I now found myself in South Carolina, at 3:00am, in the wintertime with the future unknown and no sight of anything or anyone who looked familiar. I was a kid, but in a million ways a man. I told myself I was made to do this and made to be there in this moment of time. I picked up my duffle bag from the ground from where I placed it by my feet to look around. Next, I crossed the street to the address and pinpoint which we were instructed to report on the documents mailed to us newly enlisted soldiers.

The first Drill Sergeant I met was Drill Sergeant Miriam. She would be awarded "Drill Sergeant of the Cycle" while I was there in South Carolina. Basic training is a mandatory requirement that would first need to be satisfied and completed before moving on to the next phase as to enter into the military officially. Drill Sergeant Miriam was from the Midwest, Kalamazoo to be precise. Honestly I was shocked she was a soldier. I mean she was absolutely beautiful, regal in a militant way, stoically attractive, but I would soon learn … as tough as nails. There I stood in the middle of a cold October night, with a 'bathing apes' brand hoodie on, directly from the streets of Atlanta, Georgia, not knowing what my next steps were. I crossed my arms instinctively, as I often did to anchor myself in a resting position. She immediately charged over to me and asked me "soldier do you have an attitude?" I said no ma'am! She asked, "ma'am?" and she replied to me saying, "soldier I'm nobody's ma'am… I actually work for a living! So, now you can get to the back of the food line to get some grub to eat"! I sincerely thanked her and replied back by saying "I am from Atlanta, Sergeant … so eating wasn't always guaranteed". Although she didn't reply I saw a faint smile before she turned away. At the time, I naively didn't know why I offended her or why she was taken back my ma'am reference. As any Georgian child will tell you that the only two ways to refer respectfully to any adult, is yes ma'am and yes sir. I meant no disrespect by it and felt even more out of place with this new culture shock of being thrusted into a world that I did not know and did not yet understand. Today, she is now retired Command Sergeant Major Miriam, and is a great friend! Later, I would come to learn why the ma'am comment to Command Sergeant Major Miriam, did offend and slightly amuse her. It seemed that there was a stigma in the military about Officers (Lieutenant's to Generals) "not doing any work" just sitting behind a desk all day. The Officers are called Sir's and Ma'am. The Sergeants are called "Sergeants" regardless of gender. They actually train the soldiers; they are more hands on. Calling a Sergeant, a "sir" or ma'am is a small joke.

The following next sixteen weeks of my life, I would call Foxtrot 3/60 home. Basic training taught me about reaching past my potential and exposed gifts and talents, in which before then I was unaware of. It brought me to new heights and levels of endurance and patience and each day I saw myself developing more and more into the soldier that will be required of me. I channeled my determination by watching my other fellow soldiers' attempts and failures during training and combat cycles. I quickly decided to learn to make different choices to avoid their same fate. Also teach them better ways to obtain their goals. I am a natural born leader, and a fast, practical, and visual learner. I used the same skills I quickly learned and developed to guide, teach and lead others to success. Move on a target the same way you move on a goal. Reach the target like you reach a goal. Win standing up and always finish strong! Army strong.

Being challenged was the constant norm during those sixteen weeks at winter basic training. One day, I was taking the standardized physical training test (PT Test), and I stopped after successfully completing forty-two mandated pushups, which was the minimum requirement to pass the test. The Drill Sergeant administering the test, told me to get back down and to do another ten pushups. In which I easily complied with. After completing the additional ten pushups, the Drill Sergeant commanded me to complete another ten pushups. I replied yes, "Drill Sergeant" (or Drill SGT) and easily completed the additional ten pushups. He did this until I successfully completed ninety-five pushups. That was until my arms somewhat gave out. He told me from that day forward I can only do a minimum of ninety pushups, and not one less than ninety.

It was an invaluable lesson and taught me about the unknown capabilities that we failed to tap into under the notions of compliance and societal standards. Also called "playing it safe". The Drill Sgt taught me how to challenge myself. Go for it! Go till you can't anymore in all you do. No matter what give yourself your all! I aimed for forty-two because it is what I knew I could do. Till this day I will never only do forty pushups in one sitting.

Basic Training taught me how to believe in myself plus I can do all things through Christ who strengthens me. Nothing can stop me not even me.

Sometimes, we as people do not see what we are capable of achieving, until another person allows us the privilege of seeing ourselves through their eyes. Through the same lenses, of the level of potential in which they view us in. Sometimes I pause and wonder how God views me through his eyes. I often wonder to myself at times, am I using all my gifts and talents at their maximum potential for his good and glorification?

We were peg as the "Airborne Unit" which to be honest, was never humorous to me; because of what happened one awful night at Ft. Jackson. We were returning home from Christmas and New Year's break. Even as a dedicated soldier, I always thought then and even now it was simply a bad idea for the Army to let soldiers in basic training go home for the Christmas and New Year's holiday break. When someone is in any type of training environment and are abruptly allowed to return to an environment that promotes freedom and less restrictions, giving them a taste of a level serenity and euphoria in which they were no longer accustomed to. It will whet the appetite of trainees by giving them the remembrances of the life they were use too prior to living in a concrete building being yelled at.

People would have told themselves anything to quit in order to go back to the familiarity and the life of being back at home. As soon as we all began the slow but rhythmic steps of falling back into line, the damage was already done for a few of the soldiers and basic training was no longer a once desirable rite of passage, but rather a prison and impediment to the lives that they now regretted leaving behind.

Upon returning to training, we were to report to the gun range for shooting training needed in order to pass and qualify for the weapons familiarization part of our testing and assessment. It was then, three of my friends came up with the idea and mission of collecting money in order to run away and go back home to be with their families. In other words, they were planning to go AWOL, which in the military was a serious offense and referred to the act of an individual leaving the military environment without receiving permission from their chain of command. Yet, the idea of abandonment would plague one of my friends, because it was the idea of abandonment which motivated him to get back home to his family, as he just been made aware that his wife was with child and they were going to have a baby. No longer did the army seem like a viable option for success of providing for his family in his mind, if it meant that he would have to be away from his family and miss all that he signed up to fight for. All three prematurely planned to ultimately raise enough money to purchase bus tickets from South Carolina to go home, one to Florida and the other two soldiers to two other different States. Once they obtained enough money, they would then move to execute their plans and elevate themselves to new heights.

The night my friends gathered together all of the money needed to execute their mission to escape from basic training, they also began to set forth their plans. Their plan together was to jump out of the window from the third story to the ground level unseen. After landing to the ground level unseen, they were to run to the bus station while successfully avoiding military detection the whole way.

They informed their closest friends they have gathered together all of the money required and they we're leaving that night. They said their goodbyes and set forth to start their journey to freedom. We watched them proceed with their plan, as each person went to a different window in the barracks building. To avoid any undue suspicion and avoid being caught by our Drill Sergeant. In retrospect, I could see how they thought that would make sense. Whereby, in their minds, three people jumping out of the same window would cause a ruckus and make way too much noise in one central location, whereas one person finding an available window on the same floor but at different positions in the building, would instead dispel attention and stagger the noise of someone jumping to the first floor. Well, it may have initially sounded like a good idea in their minds, but it was anything but! Each person went to their designated windows as chosen and as planned, jumped from their different window simultaneously toward what they thought would be the beginning their new lives. Home sweet home, right?

Right from the beginning, the plan was very flawed and set to fail miserably from its inception. All three lacked the logistical experience needed and the ability to conduct the viable due diligence required in assessing and calculating the distance between jumping from a third story window of a concrete building onto the ground level parking deck. Unfortunately, what the three would devastatingly discover was that the windows that they all chose to jump from, that cold night in South Carolina, overlooking the streetlights and the distance trees that rub shoulders with those same lights; where on the side of the building which the actual ground was skewed. In addition, to the fact that, the base's loading deck was actually on that side of the building, they jump from. This, added an additional ten feet to an already impossible and dangerous jump. The jump was no longer three stories high but, actually four stories, equating to about a forty-five feet jump. This was an extremely dangerous miscalculation……..

The three soldiers each sat at the window ledge that dark and cold night in South Carolina three stories up each of which looked down towards freedom and

jumped...
....BANG!

The three soldier's bodies hit the ground at a high speed. Immediately following the sounds of their bodies hitting the concrete ground were the soldiers agonizing screams. "HELP!!! HELPPPP!! PLEASEEE SOMEBODY HELP!!! ANYBODY!!! HELLLPP!!! HELPPP!!! HELLLLPP!!!! "shouted the three soldiers. The Drill Sgt. ran outside immediately upon hearing the combination of the soldier's bodies hitting the ground at breakneck speed and their screams in which succeeded the loud banging noise from the soldier's bodies. It immediately sent chills down the Drill Sgt. spine as he ran towards the screams begging to himself in his mind that these kids are ok. Upon arriving to the aid of his soldier's the Drill Sgt observed a sight in which he would never forget. Three of his soldiers unmovable from the waist down, only able to move their hands and every part of their body from the waist up. The soldiers were each in a state of hysteria, crawling backwards, and dragging their mangled legs screeching for help. "HELP!!! HELPP!! PLEASEEE ANYONEE HELP!!!" howled the soldiers. Immediately the Drill Sgt was taking back to the memory of when he was involved in an IED explosion in Iraq. He lost some of his friends that day, his determination kicked in he would not lose these kids tonight.

Remembering his training the Drill Sgt raced into action for the aid of the soldiers. The Drill Sgt completed basic level combat life saver support on each injured soldier. He started checking their pulse rate to ensure they were far from the dangers of shock. He examined their spine to ensure it wasn't broken. After angrily and lovingly holding each individual soldier ensuring to them, they would be ok, the Drill Sgt ran to call the paramedics. Afterwards, the Drill Sgt. called everyone downstairs to conduct a headcount to identify if any other soldier successfully escaped without injury. To his momentary satisfaction no other soldier tried to escape.

We all stood in unbelievable sharp formation displaying the highest level of mental discipline seeming unbothered but, mentally staying strong for our friends as they bellowed in the background.

The Drill Sgt. tore into us. "YOU HEAR THIS!" wailed the Drill Sgt. "THIS IS UNNESSARY ANYONE WHO WANTS TO LEAVE THE ARMY LEAVE NOW AND TAKE THE F**** STAIRS!! WE DO NOT WANT WEAK SOLDIERS!" Exclaimed the Drill. SGT., I did not see anything weak with their intentions. Sure, everything they thought should've been reconsider. The Army could've provided for their family of course. Nevertheless, nothing is weak about a man's desire to move his family forward by any means necessary even if it means jumping out a window to achieve it. However, I am sure they were praying to God Ahyah that they would fully recover. I am certain they were thinking no amount of money was worth them losing their ability to walk with their kids. They made a tremendous mistake.

We stood chin up, chest out, arms back, and arms fully extended down with the thumbs on the outside of the thighs. Looking straight ahead in the cold while our friends lay less than 200 meters away screaming and begging repeatedly for the units help. Twenty-five minutes later the paramedics arrived at the site of the accident and discovered the three soldiers laying in a pool of their own blood. Their legs disfigured, and their knee bones protruding through the skin of their knees. Some soldiers were crying tears of anger as they stood at the position of attention listening to their friend's screams ricocheted through the cold South Carolina, winter night, unable to assist. Others stood tall, bold, and erected, at the position of attention with their arms straight down and shoulders back, in complete and obedient silence in displaying the highest levels of military discipline. Unmoving on the outside, vicariously feeling their pain and torment on the inside. From that day forward we were referred to mockingly as, "The Airborne Unit".

I made sure to write and call home from time to time and check-in. Although, I was very cognizant in ensuring grace upon my mother, my sister, and my brother would inquire about my every moment I was experiencing during Basic Training. To minimize that, I figured I would inform them of everything that happened while I was in training after I completed it. Of course, my mother wrote me consistently while I was in Basic Training. Every mail call I would receive a handwritten letter from my mother signed "mom". I was also cognizant and mindful of staying focused and not allowing myself to be side-tracked by a world to me that seemed so far away.

One day my Drill Sgt. called me to his office. "Pvt Nunnally" yelled Drill SGT Gideon. "Moving Drill SGT.", I replied. I stepped in his office and snapped to the position of parade rest immediately. (Standard protocol when walking into a higher ranking SGT's office. I stood with my feet shoulder length apart and my hands interlock. My right hand is placed on top of my left hand with both hands comfortably resting in the small of my lower back.) "Nunnally, we are going to make you Bay Leader for 3rd Platoon. You are responsible for your soldiers in your platoon who sleeps in the bay. If they need anything make sure you get it for them and if you cannot resolve it, then find one of us." Explained Drill Sgt. Gideon. "Roger that Drill Sgt". I stated. "You are dismiss." said Drill Sgt. Gideon. "Thank you Drill Sgt., I stated. Afterwards I snapped back to the position of attention from parade rest, conducted an about face, and walked out his office. (Again, standard protocol). With my responsibilities increasing as I was newly appointed as Bay Leader. I now had to identify the proper way to command the respect and authority over sixty different personalities. A talent needed in the business world, how do you manage your subordinates. My first question I asked myself was. "What is the best way for a leader to lead? Through fear and rulership? or through respect and admiration? Maybe every situation is different?"

Nevertheless, upon being newly appointed to the position as "bay leader". I met Isaac, a soldier from Chicago. Isaac and I stood at roughly the same height at 5'10. He was dark skin with a muscular build around 180 pounds. Isaac sense of humor was without a doubt unmatched. He was a Master Barber, and his title was well deserved. He perfected his talent. We became really good friends, and he definitely made a lot of money in the bay from cutting hair. We made a bet to see which one of us would make the most money by the end of the cycle. He made roughly $5,000 extra from cutting hair in the bay while the bay leader was away. That wasn't enough of course…not even close. Nevertheless, when the opportunity presented itself to me to start making money in Basic Training, I would take it. The opportunity did come in the most uncomfortable manner as it normally does.

On, the last month of basic training we were told we could walk to the PX (which was the name of the military grocery store, on post) to purchase cellphones to call home. Two other soldiers and I walked politely to the PX in line formation or (single filed line) to obtain our new cellphones from the PX. Out of nowhere a Drill Sergeants marching his unit stopped in front of us. "Soldiers" said the Drill SGT. "Yes Drill SGT" we replied in harmony. "Where are you going?" questioned the Drill SGT. Without the presences of a Drill SGT. it was against Army Regulation for any trainee to travel away from our quarters. I looked at the Drill Sgt.'s name tagged it said Potiphar. Drill Sgt. Potiphar was country he spoke with a heavy accent. His vernacular carried a southern draw but not one identifiable to what I am accustom to back home. The Drill Sgt automatically concluded we were attempting to go AWOL. He commanded us to fall in with his unit and he marched us back to our quarters.

Drill Sergeant Gideon and Drill Sgt Rueben were sitting outside on the black top while we approached them marching in formation with Drill Sgt Potiphar and his company. "Platoon,. Halt!" exclaimed Drill SGT Potiphar followed with his command of "Right….Face." "Too smooth!" proclaimed his platoon all in unison. I was impressed but, my unit was better of course. Drill Sgt Potiphar immediately singled identified us by yelling." My three runaway soldiers fall out of formation and stand fast I will walk you to your Drill Sgt." "Moving Drill SGT." we all yell back. We stood outside of formation quietly awaiting Drill Sgt Potiphar's orders. He walked over to us and motioned us to follow him by waving his hand as he walked passed. We all complied. He asked "Which Drill Sgt were we assigned too?" I told him "Drill Sgt. Rueben and Drill Sgt Gideon." Drill SGT Potiphar approached Drill Sgt Gideon and said," I found three of your strays trying to run away, I figured I would bring them back to their rightful owner." "I got your stray thought to myself. "Drill Sgt. Gideon looked at us extremely disappointed and demanded we report outside his office. "Roger, Drill Sgt. We all stated." Drill Sgt.

Gideon wrapped up his conversation with Drill Sgt. Potiphar and he stormed into his office. "NUNNALLY, YOU IN MY OFFICE FIRST!" I took a deep breath and thought to myself, lets hurry up and get this over with.

"Nunnally!" yelled Drill Sgt. Gideon. "What did you learn in Basic Training!" he blasted. "Teamwork, mental strength, courage, and loyalty," I replied back "Stealth Nunnally! Learn how to move in silence in broad day light! Apparently, you need to master the night first" I was not expecting this honestly. I knew he could not be upset that we were going to the PX but I did not know that he wasn't supposed too. I was glad I didn't tell Drill Sgt. Potiphar we received permission to go he wouldn't have believed us anyway. Nevertheless, Drill Sgt. Gideon was teaching me a different lesson altogether. "Move in silence during the daytime under stealth another way to looking at it is do not let your right hand know what your left hand is doing. "Nunnally!" Exclaimed Drill SGT Gideon, he proceeded with "Your corrective action for this infraction is to go to the PX and come back here without being detected and without getting caught. To ensure that you have successfully complied with my corrective action terms and in order to prove you have successfully completed this task, bring me back a pack of Twizzlers. In addition to that you will write up an 'Op Order' as well. (Op order, being short for operations order explains how to plan and execute the mission). I replied, "Yes, Drill Sergeant", and snapped back to the position of attention from parade rest, conducted an about face, and walked out his office. That night in the bay, I immediately began planning my trip to the PX and how I would execute Drill Sergeant commands and proof of success.

Nighttime at Ft. Jackson began usually when the sun sets around 7:00 pm. The PX closed its door at 9:00 pm sharp. This only allotted me a two-hour window to execute the operation without any hiccups, hesitations, or delays. My bay was located on the third floor. Regardless of how brazen I am, walking out the front door without detection was impractical. The Drill Sgt's night guard desk was downstairs. His position at the front door positioned him to face North. His back was turned against the stairs that led up to the bays. Walking out the front stairs, I would pass his office on my right side and be in his field of vision for at least forty to fifty seconds. His visual vantage point was able to overlook the blacktop, the door from the back stairs, and the walkway for approaching visitors coming to our unit. The thought of jumping out the window was inconceivable and the nightmares from the three soldier's scream's still plague my mind. Nevertheless, the backdoor stairs across the blacktop which faces the front door of the Drill Sgt desk appears to be the only logical choice.

The next day after lights out Drill Sgt Smith was on duty. I knew the risk was greater taking a chance of this magnitude while another Drill Sgt was on duty and not Drill Sgt Gideon. I preferred Drill Sgt Gideon. I knew the satisfaction of achieving glory while he was on duty in particular would be more gratifying. Even he would not expect me to strike the next day. However, regardless of who is on duty it was time to put my operation into motion! Since I was the bay leader, I placed a friend of mine named Mark on night guard. Mark was from Oklahoma and poised a calm demeanor. I inform him to let me know when the Drill Sgt was in his office. He acknowledges and obliged. I told him unfortunately we lacked communications without a cellphone or a walkie talkie device we will have to fly blind on this journey.

I quickly went down the back stairs and approached the back door extremely slowly. I lightly pressed my finger on the door and as light as I possibly could, I pushed opened the door to try to hear any movement.........silence. Next, I slightly peaked only my right eye to the opening of the door......clear. No sign of Drill Sgt Smith. It was maybe fifteen feet to the corner of the building. I felt the cold breeze of the South Carolina night air kiss my face sending tingles throughout my skin. My breath rose up as a mist before my eyes. I could make out my next move through the smoke in my breath. As soon as I inhale next, I will hold my breath and start this mission with a quiet but quick and efficient dash to the entrance way on my tip toes. I exhaled one one thousand, two one thousand, I inhale again and held my breath. I leapt from behind the door and landed on my tip toes. With my right arm against the brick wall, I hopped again and landed on my left foot, before my foot solidified contact amongst the ground I leaped again and took the corner.

Once I took the corner I allowed my back and the brick building to hug as I side stepped in the shadow area of the visitors walk way. It was dark outside of course and I knew I had only 1 hour and 45 minutes to get to the PX, which was still ultimately one mile away on foot.

I ran across the field I knew I had to get out of the battalion's view just in case one of our many Drill Sergeants, decided to casually look out of the window. I hugged the tree line on the way to the PX. My vision levels were normal for nighttime seeing. I could see maybe about 300 yards ahead, as it was a dark and clear night in South Carolina. As I was jogging to the PX, in order to keep within the allotted time frame of getting to the PX successfully before they closed. My heart was racing as I thought to myself I joined the Army to never have to take risks again, now I am taking one of the biggest risk in my life with my life. I would periodically see cars coming down the road and would have to immediately drop down as low as I possibly could to break outside of their view according to their direction and position while traveling. I would hide in the dark enclosures of the woods. Once certain the cars had passed by, I would wait for their taillights to completely disappear into the darkness. Next, I would bravely emerge again and continue down the road, ever so determined to accomplish this quest that I'd already irrevocably began. Walking low to the ground and at a fast pace, I am maybe 500 meters to the target of reaching the PX, before closing. 200 meters away is the last obstacle, the PX itself. I made it!

When I observed the parking lot, I almost felt defeated. It was infested with Drill Sergeants and permanent soldiers. If one of these individuals identify me correctly that's the end of the mission and my five-month career with the Army. That will not happen I made it too far that wasn't an option for me. I abruptly removed my patrol cap from the crown of my head then replaced it with my Army issued beret. "Stealth in the night" I said to myself and I walked boldly and confidently inside of the PX. With my heart beating a million miles per minute in my chest, but not showing it, I decided to go on a shopping spree. I grabbed a buggy and went down aisle after aisle obtaining items, I believed soldiers would want in the barracks. I purchased tobacco dip, cellphones, two burgers from burger king, skittles, twixs, sneakers candy, and other contrabands. I turn down the next aisle and there it was the twizzlers for Drill Sgt. Gideon. After obtaining the main mission I proceeded to check out. "Good evening Pvt Nunnally did you find everything alright? "the lady asked. "Yes, I did" I replied. "Ok that would be $67.68" I calmly swiped my debt card and thanked the cashier kindly. I turned and walked out of the PX. As soon as I walked out of sight, I secured everything I purchased into the assault pack. Next, I asked God to protect me on the journey back to the barracks.

As I began my way back to the barracks, it was a miniature hill in front of me. I walked to the top of the hill. I was making sure to use the same unspoken trail I came. My focus could only be described as stealth with laser precision. As I started my slight jog, I chose to jog one inch inside the wood line the whole route, as not to be detected by anyone coming from behind me. I could hear the crickets in the distance and smell the crisp clear nighttime air mix in with the combination of pine trees. While I was jogging through the wood lines at a normal pace and hopping over branches on the floor of the woods while simultaneously sprinting pass the pine combs that were attached to them. I was thinking, I hope I can pull this off successfully, and I also hope Drill Sgt Gideon did not set me up. However, the goal was to get back to the barracks before the Drill Sergeant performed their bay checks. I came up to a crossing and emerged from the wood line. I looked to the right and then the left. I neither heard nor seen any sign of a vehicle. All clear! Next, I focused into the wood line across the street to identify a place in which I felt comfortable darting to. "I only need to be in the wood lines two inches" I told myself. I look to the right and the left again and pierced the wood line with sheer speed. Once I was back in the wood line, I kept up the pace again. Jumping and hopping over branches hearing the candy rattling in the bag. Finally, the barracks came into view. First sign of a mission complete. I quickened my jog, still keeping in mind that I had everything to lose if discovered, and made my way back to the part of the wall on the visitors walkway. The Drill Sergeant desk were now looking like enemies to me. I sidestepped slowly controlling my breathing to the edge of the barracks and peaked over. It was clear! Next, I turn the corner and walked back to the door in which I started the mission. The door opened up and I walked in. As soon as the door closed I gave out a sigh of relief. "Second sign of being clear." I said to myself. "However, let's make sure the Drill Sgt. did not check the barracks." I continued up the stairs and opened the door. Mark was still on guard duty. I gave him a burger for his hard work. I sold to my fellow enlistees the rest of the goodies. Bags of skittles, was suddenly worth $20 and tobacco dip sold for an upward of $50, due to demand. I made over $500 for my first run to the PX. Not bad for an enlistee, determination meets entrepreneurship, risk and reward.

The next day Drill Sgt Gideon called me back into his office. "Good job, Private Nunnally." He said eating a twizzler in his mouth. "Now that you know how to successfully execute this mission, and you can move in the dark apply what you learn in the day time. Also only leave, and go to the PX when someone in your bay under your care is in great need …not for your greed". I replied to him,

"Roger that, Drill Sergeant". I found a way to challenge Isaac and help people.

The next day while I was outside with two other soldiers from my unit in the visitor's walkway Drill Sgt. Potiphar (also a biblical name google it) recognized me from walking us back to the unit. "If it isn't the runaway from the Airborne Unit." Said Drill Sgt. Potiphar. "I don't see anything funny with that at all Drill Sgt." I stated. "I do." said Drill Sgt. Potiphar. "That's flaw." I said "Flaw!" Drill Sgt. Potiphar. "Yes Drill Sgt." I stated. "Where you from Nunnally?" asked Drill Sgt. Potiphar. "Atlanta" I replied. "We the same Nunnally." Replied Drill Sgt. Potiphar. "I beg to defer" I replied "Where I'm from my people won't find three teenagers jumping out of a window humors." I responded. "Where are you from Drill Sgt?" I asked. "Little Rock, Arkansas" stated Drill Sgt. Potiphar. "oh yeah, like the television show banging in little rock?" I replied. "Yes," he replied zealously. "Yeah, sorry to burst bubble homeboy but again where I'm from we wouldn't find it funny for three teenagers to break their kneecaps we are not the same and banging in Little rock was a television show Atlanta is a real life Drill Sgt.

"GET DOWN AND PUSH UNTIL THE CLOUDS GET SWEATY!!" Drill Sgt. Potiphar. "Sure", I responded it was worth it. Just then Drill Sgt Rueben observed what was happening she ran over to us. "Nunnally, get up" said Drill Sgt. Rueben. "I stood up. Drill Sgt Rueben asked me "Nunnally, what happen?" said Drill SGT Reuben. "The Drill Sgt was making fun of our soldiers jumping out the window, I am loyal to my team." I stated. She told me to report to the unit and I obliged.

True to form, the next time I made a store run was when a friend of mine injured his leg and needed an icy hot to cool the pain at night, and no longer was I in the convenience store consignment business.

Graduating from Basic Training and beating Isaac was a milestone. After basic training I decided to switch from Army Reserve to Army Active Duty as soon as I graduated from A.I.T. However, I was curious since I did receive a bonus when I joined the Army Reserve.

After Basic Training was Advanced Individual Training (or AIT). In which I stayed at Fort Jackson, South Carolina. Finally out of the cold in

Fort Jackson, it was now March and we were arriving into spring. Personnel who were staying at Fort Jackson South Carolina were ordered to step aside and load the bus that would take us to the A.I.T. side of post. From my window on the bus I could see the A.I.T. barracks coming into view. The bus turned into the driveway of the barracks and we departed from the bus very similar to how we departed from Basic Training. We all grabbed our duffle bags and stepped off the bus. A Sgt greeted us and assigned us to our barracks room. The barracks room we stayed at, in A.I.T were smaller than the ones in Basic Training. These barracks room only held eight soldiers in the room. Four on one side and four on the other. "PVT Nunnally, this is your barrack room." Stated the SGT. "Roger, SGT" I replied. All eight of us entered the room who were assigned to the barracks. "Was anyone the bay leader in this room from Basic Training?" asked the SGT. "Not this time" I thought to myself. I will get some sleep during this phase of training. It was quiet "Ok" said the Sgt. He went around the room and asked everyone where they were from. He came to me. "Nunnally, where are you from?" asked the SGT.

"Atlanta." I responded. "You're bay leader, Nunnally." "Roger Sgt." I responded.

When I arrived to my unit, I no longer desired to become a mechanic anymore. After tasting Basic Training, I wanted to become an Infantryman. I was informed I would have to send in a request to my 1sgt. (1st Sergeant means the highest-ranking Sergeant in the company). 1SGT Julian who I was going to meet the next day. I went to dinner by myself that night to think about goals for the future. I also wanted to think about if I made a good decision or not. The next day I met our 1sgt Julian, he was an old school corvette driver he loved his cars. I reported to his office. "1SGT Julian" I stated, "Who is it and what do you want?" he replied. "My name is PVT Nunnally and I want to reclass to Infantry 1SGT". "Nunnally, nobody likes to get shot at for fun" he replied. At that moment another Sgt entered the office he added, "High speed, I lost three inches off my height from jumping out of airplanes for the infantry. It was fun when I was young but my body paid for it when I got older." he said. My attempt to go infantry was rejected.

Our unit was called "Mad Dogs" our mascot was a glass dog. 1SGT Julian had a game he liked to play in which he would assign the mascot to a soldier for the day. One day during formation 1SGT Julian called me to the front of formation. "Nunnally, front and center!" proclaimed 1Sgt Julian. "Moving 1SGT". I yelled. I stepped out of formation and ran to 1sgt Julian. I render a salute and stated. "1SGT Julian, PVT Nunnally reporting as order." 1Sgt Julian saluted back and stated "PVT Nunnally, today is your day to escort the Mascot."

"Roger that, 1SGT Julian". I dropped my salute and picked up the Mascot. Upon returning to formation a soldier stepped and accidently hit the glass dog out my hand and the mascot shattered into pieces. 1SGT Julian hollered. "PVT NUNNALLY FRONT AND CENTER!" "I responded "Moving 1SGT." "Nunnally you killed the dog!" stated 1SGT Julian. "Roger top" I said. "Nunnally you need to dig a hole and bury the dog to ensure he goes to heaven" said 1sgt Julian. 1SGT Julian held the unit outside while I dug a hole for the glass dog. After I completed digging the whole I placed the glass pieces into the hole.

"Nunnally!" yelled 1SGT Julian "Yes 1SGT" I replied "Say some words for the dog." " Roger top." I responded "And cry!" he said. I fake cried the whole time I gave kind words to an inanimate object. "Nunchucks" 1SGT Julian said. I gave him a stare of confusion. "Your new name is Nunchucks" said 1SGT. That was my first week of A.I.T.

Upon graduating A.I.T. I headed back to Atlanta, Georgia. I was so excited about my experience being in Basic Training that Atlanta was no longer fulfilling. I yearned to travel more, I wanted to see new things, and meet new people. For the first time in my life Atlanta was small to me. I needed something different. The urge to travel, grow, learn, explore, taste new food, and experience new experiences was screaming inside of me. The Army woke up a new desire I did not know I had. I reported to my unit in Decatur Georgia. I reported to my Colonel's Office, (His name is Colonel Lewis), to switch over to Army Active Duty. He was the only person who could sign off on the paperwork for me to switch over to Active Duty. "Sir." I stated. "Yes" replied Colonel Lewis "I would like to switch over to Army Active Duty." I replied. "I love when soldiers go active duty, I see you have a $30,000 sign on bonus for the Army Reserve. If you switch over to Army Active Duty you will have to pay back the $30,000 they will take it from your check. Do you still want to join the Army Active Duty? "asked Colonel Lewis. I weighted my options; I could stay in Atlanta with $30,000 or pay back the $30,000 and experience new experiences in life. I chose to switch pay back the $30,000 bonus and switch to Army Active Duty. I switched the same day.

Two months later, I received a call from my recruiter. "PVT Nunnally, since you are switching over to Active Duty, where would you like to be stationed at?" asked my recruiter. "Anywhere overseas" I told her. I knew leaving it in the hands of the Army, I was going to be assigned to the next unit deploying to Iraq, but I was perfectly ok with the decision. She said ok and assigned me to Germany. "Nunnally you will report to Germany by way of South Carolina." Said my recruiter. Then we hung up the phone. My ship off day back to South Carolina and ultimately to Germany was only a month away. As a teenager from Atlanta,

Georgia, directly from Basic Training, October would have a profound meaning in my life as it relates to travel and winter. I would again arrive in a foreign place in the month of October, in the cold of their winter.

Upon reporting for duty and signing the necessary paperwork I would receive $15,000 as a sign-on bonus from the Army. I received an additional $15,000, as well. In total I would receive $30,000 to enlist in the Army for four years. The thrill and excitement of it all. I opened up two Roth IRA accounts one for five years and one for ten. The next pay check I received from the Army was $100.00 a month until I paid back my signing bonus to the Army Reserve. Until I redeployed from Iraq the Army would take 80% of my check while I was 18 years old in Germany. I would only receive my full check from the Army after I redeployed from Iraq.

As a newly arrived soldier, to Germany I arrived to Frankfurt Airport. A Sergeant welcomed us with open arms to Germany. He said "Nunnat nun.." "Nunnally," I interrupted. "Right, welcome Nunnally." Responded the Sgt. "You can have a seat with the rest of the soldiers and wait till you hear your name." he continued. I sat and waited with the rest of the soldiers as we waited patiently for our orders. I watched some television and was amazed at all the different types of people who traveled to Germany. It was my first time ever leaving the country. "PVT Nunnally" stated the SGT. "Moving Sgt." I responded. "Fall in" he added. He ordered everyone else to fall in by alphabetical order. Next, he went to the front of the line and started with the "A's" assigning soldiers to their units. "Grafenwohr, Grafenwohr, Grafenwohr," he proceeded down the line. "Darmstadt, Darmstadt, Darmstadt" continued the Sgt. "Baumholder, Baumholder, Baumholder". He came to me "Wiesbaden", he pointed at the person behind me "Baumholder", "Baumholder", as he continued through the rest of the soldiers. I was the only person in the chalk assigned to Wiesbaden. I was told by the Sergeant , "Nunnally you are going to report to the 501st Military Police Company (MP)." I would later learn that I was the only person assigned to the Military Police, that day. I was confused nevertheless, with $30,000 in my account that I knew I had to pay back I had other things on my mind.

When I arrived at my unit, they were in Iraq. I stayed in the rear with the rest of the soldiers who did not deploy. I met a Sgt name Sgt Esau. Sgt Esau was from Ghana. He was a great person with an amazing personality. He stood maybe 6'4. He towered over me and the other soldiers. Nevertheless, we were placed on all detail with three others soldiers every time. Two were from Ghana, and one African American woman from North Carolina, who was also a friend.

One day while we all stood outside in formation. Sgt Esau was called to the office. We all waited for him to return. After ten minutes, he emerged. "Company" yelled Sgt Esau. "Attention" we all snapped to attention. "Sgt. Tarshish. fall out and report to the CQ area." stated Sgt. Esau. "The rest of you report to the empty barracks for clean-up detail." proclaimed Sgt Esau. One of the other Sgt who was ordered to fall out name was Sgt Moore. Sgt Moore was from South Dakota he was very calm, and medium built. He is a bless man who survived over five IED explosions in Iraq. He was younger than SGT Esau in both age and rank. At that time, I wondered why he was never on details with us Nevertheless, I chose to stay in my lane, that is the best way to avoid accidents. We were instructed to shovel snow, clean barracks, and connexs. I humbly obliged. The other soldiers who were instructed to fall out were drinking coffee in the office while we would go into the thick in the snow to perform our detail, while they conveniently and luxuriously sat in his office drinking coffee. I knew something was wrong and I knew that these weren't mere coincidences, but I also felt that this battle may be above my pay grade, so I stayed clear. Yet, a close friend of mine and soldier named Paul, didn't feel that my battle was above his pay grade. He was Caucasian, a great guy had a sense of integrity that I wish more people aspired to and was a great man of Faith. He believed that having three minorities standing outside in the snow for a detail, without proper clothing and without merit was arbitrary, capricious, and downright was discriminatory. In protest he would come outside with us every time we were on snow detail, and prove a point and stand outside with us, regardless of the taunting of the other Caucasian sergeants telling him that he didn't have to stay outside in the cold and snow with us.

It wouldn't be until years later, speaking with him and catching up that he would finally admit to me that it made him mad so much, that he went to one of our Commanding Officers to tell him that how we were being treated as minorities soldiers, was downright inhumane, uncalled for and didn't look good for the Army.

If I didn't love and respect him already as a brother and confidant, his admission of standing up for me and the other soldiers would make my chest swell with admiration and esteem I always held for him! I was an E-2 at the time and I only just wanted to do the best I could do no matter the task. Paul told me that good just make sure you do the best you can do on the right side of things.

As if I may have already been thinking that these acts of mistreatments were racially charged and discriminatory, I knew for sure that when another sergeant, Sergeant Miller came to me one day and told me that I was not allowed to literally speak to anyone that was not in my immediate unit. Although, that seemed somewhat extreme and went against the instinctive throbbing and prudent reasoning I felt in my head, I complied and acknowledged his command. He also added that I was to, "always stay out of the EAC", which was basically an area a soldier would go if they were on 24-hour duty. Again, I complied and responded, "Roger Sergeant". No reasons given, no explanations, no apparent punishment due to something I did wrong but rather just two arbitrary and capricious commands that would encapsulate me as a new soldier in seclusion, ridicule, mistreatment, and isolation.

Soon after that, I would meet a Chief Warrant Officer, who I immediately came to admire and appreciate the way that Chief Warrant Officer carried himself, operated as an Officer and how he treated others. In the military there are three routes of promotions you can climb. Enlisted, which takes you from Private to Command Sergeant Major. Officer, which takes you from 2nd Lieutenant to four Star General. Then you have Warrant Officer (who is the 14th rank in the United States Army, above any of the Sergeant Majors), which requires that you have to first be enlisted and then changed over at the rank of E-4 (the highest rank for junior enlisted recruits), before then becoming CW1 to CW5 (which stands for Warrant Officers).

As a stickler for rules and regulations, I was very enthralled with rank, protocol, and procedures, and respecting the rules and regulations indoctrinated into us and always required of us as provided in our protocol manuals, received upon arrival. Such an appreciation for rules and regulations, normally would be thought to be a great trait for a soldier in the United States Army.

Keeping that in mind, one day the Chief Warrant Officer (who outranked everyone in my chain of command) instructed me to go down to the EAC to use its phone to call him. I replied, "Roger Chief Warrant Officer", and immediately ran to the EAC and to call him from a phone there, as requested. He picked up right away, he told me good job and stayed on the phone to tell me how I could one day too become a Chief Warrant Officer. I was truly elated and felt good not only doing something for someone I revered but finally seen as something more than an insignificant soldier only used and suitable to stand in the snow. This is the patriarchal guidance, mentorship, and camaraderie that I was seeking and expecting when initially joining the Army. I was hopeful and smiling when on the phone, and was just preparing to leave the EAC, but not before bumping into Sergeant Miller. When I saw his apparent rage and pupils dilating, my short-lived euphoric hope disappeared, and my smile was instantly non-existent.

Right away, he furiously commanded me to "come outside". As soon as I stepped outside and stopped in formation, he walked up to me with his nose almost touching mine and yelled at me that I was to drop and do pushups until my arms hurt. Fortunately, for me the Army Regulation stated soldiers who have a PT Test within 24 hours are to only do stretches. I confidently informed Sergeant Miller, "No Sergeant, I cannot drop and do pushups, Sergeant". If his eyes were dilated before at my response, this time they were almost completely black, and he yelled at me ruthlessly using profane words to intimidate into something I already knew that I couldn't do.

He again stepped up to me, nose to nose and cussed me out and said, " I want this piece of S*** out my Army". He told me to follow him to SFC (Sergeant First Class) Jethro office, and so I did!

As soon as the door closed behind us both, he threw one of the chairs across in an effort to display his unfounded temper and his unsuccessful attempt to intimidate me, but I didn't even blink when the chair crashed against the wall.

From behind the table SFC Jethro calmly, asked what happened? SSG Miller told him he gave me a direct order not to be in the EAC. SFC Jethro asked why I was in the EAC, against direct orders from Sergeant Miller. I quickly explained to him respectively, that Chief Warrant Officer explicitly gave me orders to go down to the EAC and to call from the phone within the EAC Office. SFC Jethro then asked why I didn't just explain this to Sergeant Miller when he asked me why I was in the EAC. Which I again respectfully replied, "this is the first time anyone asked me the reason why I was in the EAC".

After that incident, I immediately filed an EO complaint, which in the United States Army was any complaint premised on racial discrimination, etc). My complaint was specifically against SSG Miller and the Army agreed that his conduct against me was less than honorable and warranted and he was ultimately demoted and reranked. After that incident and the Army's finding I had no other issues of hazing and harassment from him. In fact, when the smoke cleared from that unfortunate series of events, my experience with the Military Police took an amazing turn for the best moving forward and was actually a blast. One thing about the Military Police…they definitely knew how to have fun.

With past hurdles gone and no longer being subjected to discriminatory hazing, I ended up being on the commandant and the Division Color Guard team. I would receive a total of distinctive four awards and nine coins for being on the color guard team. Yet, it came to the attention of an officer and the Army ended up finding out that I in fact had scoliosis at a 32degree curve in my spine. I was told I would be subjected to a thorough physical and would have to go through a medical board evaluation. I was lost for words. One day I went to the DFAC (dinning facility) with some friends for lunch. As I was walking, I noticed a Black Old School Corvette in the parking lot. We went into the DFAC gathered our lunches and took a seat. While I was eating, I looked up and noticed a face I have not seen since South Carolina. 1SGT

Julian. I stood up immediately and went to 1SGT Julian. "1SGT Julian!" I stated and gave him hug. "How are you doing? when did you get here?" I asked. I looked at his rank and noticed 1SGT Julian was promoted to SGM (Sergeant Major) Julian he was an E-9. (Only achieved by less than 1% of all the Army personnel. It is a huge accomplishment to become an SGM. I am blessed to know some great SGM's.) I immediately snapped to the position of Parade rest, since we were in public. "Relax Nunchucks" SGM Julian replied. "Nunchucks I thought you were Army Reserve." "SGM Julian inquired. "I changed over when I returned home and now, I am here SGM." I stated. "Nunchucks, I am happy you made that decision."

The day of my Medical Evaluation Board, I was extremely nervous. Our unit was conducting Division Safety Day and I was tapped to host it with another soldier. I spoke against drunk driving. In the middle of our break, I was ordered to report to Medical Board to hear my fate in the Army. Upon arriving at the Board, I knocked on the door. "Enter" yelled someone from behind the door. With my heart beating extremely fast I opened the door. I entered the medical board and rendered a salute. "PVT Nunnally, reporting to the Medical Board as ordered." I stated. My doctor Colonel Harper was also at the medical board. "Nunnally, I am looking at your x-rays how did you get into the Army?" Colonel Harper asked. "I went to MEPS and they cleared me duty sir" "I stated. As I looked at everyone on my Medical Board, I notice a familiar face. "Nunnally, yes SGM" I responded. "How many push-ups did you do in A.I.T?" "97 SGM Julian". "How what was your 2 mile run time Nunnally?" ask SGM Julian. "14:00 minutes SGM." I stated. "How many sit ups did you do and who was your first sergeant in A.I.T.?" I did 107 sit-ups SGM and you were my 1sgt in A.I.T. Immediately the room went silent as everyone looked at SGM Julian. "Nunnally, the way you performed in A.I.T. I had no idea you had scoliosis now I am even more happy I did not let you switch over to Infantry in A.I.T." added SGM. The medical board asked me what I would like to do. I explained to the Army's medical board, that I wanted to stay in the Army, but also mentioned to them that when it is my time to leave the Army, I would not have a say so in it. I was ready to accept my fate whichever decision came from their medical evaluation. The Medical Board found me fit for duty but nondeployable. I was temporarily happy and returned back to the Safety Stand Down Day. Safe in Germany to make more experiences while still receiving $100.00 a month.

On a warm and soft night in Germany I awoke to laughter from the back of the barracks, directly outside my window. I looked out and witness roughly seven members of the Military Police Company outside laughing drinking alcohol. As I rose up, I put on my clothes and ventured outside to obtain a closer view. Immediately as I opened the back door of the barracks, I heard someone yell loudly, "Yoooo Nunnally CHECK THIS OUT!! Yelled one of the soldiers. "It was SPC Timothy and SPC Anthony I knew it was going to be something absolutely ridiculous. They are both from the State of Texas, they both are Military Police Officers, roommates, drinking partners, they came from basic training together, and they are really good friends. My natural response back was "Yoo what's going on?" I walked over to them and was caught completely off guard with what I discovered. The soldiers had balloons at 11:30 pm at night. "What is this about?" I thought to myself.

One soldier had a radio in his hand. The voice came over the radio said, "Mad Dog One this is Mad Dog Two I have eyes on the next target." I approached them closer to get a better comprehension of what was unfolding before my eyes. "What are these MP's doing now", I asked myself. I knew it had to be something completely irresponsible yet fun in nature. "Roger that Mad Dog Two, we are loading up the ammo now." Replied Timothy. "Ammo? I thought to myself. As I walked closer, I finally caught a complete grasp of what was before my eyes.

We were positioned behind the barracks in the parking lot. One soldier held a portion of a large rubber band in one hand, the other soldier stood adjacent to him and stretched the rubber band approximately five feet. SPC Timothy poured alcohol in the balloon, tied a knot at the stem of the balloon, and loaded the balloon to the middle portion of the rubber band. Afterwards he grabbed the walkie talkie and stated, "Mad Dog Two, this is Mad Dog One we are ready to engage."

"Mad Dog One this is Mad Dog Two the target is approaching the first marker……standby and wait for my command" said the voice on the radio.

"That's a good copied" replied SPC Timothy. I reached over and grab a cup out of the mini cooler on the ground completely enthralled to what I was witnessing. I put two ice cubes in my cup and discharged a portion of their alcohol into the cup I was holding then I re-engaged the scene. "The target is less than ten feet from the marker, fire away and aim high" stated the soldier on the walkie talkie. "Roger that" stated Timothy, he received his marching orders. SPC Timothy gazed at his friend to his right then his friend to the left and stated, "let's go boys". They replied back "let's do it!" The two soldiers held on the large rubber band while SPC Timothy adjusted the rubber band slightly upward. He then placed the balloon filled with alcohol in the middle of the rubber band, next he took three large steps backwards and released the balloon. Fissssssssssssssst! whistled the balloon. My eyes locked on to the alcohol filled balloon as I watched it slowly twirled mimicking the Earth on its axes. The alcohol filled balloon ascended upward more until it reached its peak over the

building, next the balloon started to decline till it disappeared out of my sight and peacefully glided towards its unexpected target. ……splash!
The unexpected by passer yelled out "WHAT THE!" A very appropriate respond. The balloon found its target. The soldiers burst out in high fives and cheers as the radio stated, "That's a good hit Mad Dog One". We all laughed extremely genuine tears of joy and made great memories and experiences that night as 18-year-old teenagers in Germany.

That is what life is about. The memories you make with the good people in life. No matter if they are in your life for one month, one year, one decade, or if it's the one person in your life for one lifetime forever. Make the most of that time with those people. Memories are worth more than diamonds and gold. Memories create more memories when you share them with love ones. To be transparent, even today if I was offered the opportunity I would return to Germany with my same unit. With or without pay or bonus to relive those same memories with my brothers in the 501st Military Police Company. Money cannot buy memories and who knew I would have so much fun with the Police. Do not be afraid to move outside of your comfort zone to find joy.

Change, Evolve, or Both?

One day I was on a phone call with my ex-wife and, she stated she will never get married again due to me filing for a divorce. I informed her; marriages are a beautiful thing when done the correct way. Do not let our mistake, change your goal in life or your personality. Give your good traits and goals to the person who matches it. Evolve your thinking on marriages and do it the right way. Don't change your mind on marriages or your personality traits to "protect yourself" and end up losing your identity and your happiness.

Reminiscing upon my Germany days from how they began, until when the Army permanently changed my duty station, I am elated I did not allow Sgt. Miller to change my perception of the Army. In retrospect, he caused me to love the Army even more to the point I could not wait to deploy. Due to the fact I have scoliosis, the Army said I was unfit to deploy to Iraq. I visited a great friend of mine named SGM Julian again and explained to him I wanted to deploy to Iraq. SGM Julian said "Nunchuks we at full strength without you on the manifest. You would need to find someone to switch with." "Roger that SGM" I stated. "I had no idea how to even start searching nor how to open up the conversation." I thought to myself "How would someone ask a person if they can switch with them to go fight a war in Iraq when everyone believes it's such an honor to complete?" Let's see what God has in store for me and can my request be honored?

"We just redeployed I have two fifteen-month deployments under my belt and we have to deploy again!!" SPC Baker exclaimed angerly upon receiving his orders. "I think I found my way in Iraq" I thought to myself. "SPC Baker" I called out. "What Nunnally!" He responded. SPC Miller and I never were on the same page. In my opinion he was a suck up in his opinion I was from Atlanta and we were both correct. SPC Baker wrote many counseling statements against me but was happy when I was around.

Nevertheless, we have a mutual desire. He is the shop foreman meaning, he is the immediate supervisor, due to his position he has no other choice but to deploy to Iraq. No way around it unless a SGM gives the greenlight. Thank God I have access to a SGM as a E-2 in the Army, it was extremely rare. Nevertheless, based off the disgust in his voice on how he said my name, I should let him go on the deployment and find someone else who will be more appreciated of this opportunity I thought to myself. However, one bird in the hand is always better then two birds in the tree.

"Can I replace you on this deployment?" I asked "Absolutely" he responded! "Can you make that happen?" exclaimed SPC Baker. "I cannot but God blessed me to run into my old 1sgt from AIT. His name is SGM Julian. He said if I find someone to switch with then I can deploy." I inform him. "Nunnally don't toy with me like this" responded SPC Baker. "We both know I don't toy with people, meet me here tomorrow at 11:00 am and we will go visit SGM Julian and put in the request." I added. SPC Baker humbly obliged.

The next day I met with SPC Baker and we walked to visit SGM Julian. Even though he is a dear friend of mine in public I knew never to show the friendship side publicly. I only show the Army respect side, the way I want people to treat my friends as well. Regardless, of how much we respected each other and his rank of course. I knocked on the door and immediately snapped to parade rest. SPC Baker followed. We waited outside his door for almost two minutes while he was finishing up a call. "Enter!" proclaimed SGM Julian. We snapped to the position of attention and enter SGM Julian's office.

He sat behind a large size Cherokee red wood desk. Right behind him was a typical German style window with two levers in which to lock and unlock the window. The window viewed the parking lot and the food court across the street from his building. SGM Julian was sitting at his desk when SPC Baker and I walked in. I snapped to the position of attention and rendered the most prestigious salute just like he verified in A.I.T. I then said in the most command voice I can muster, "SGM Julian, Private Nunnally and SPC Baker reporting as requested SGM." SGM Julian looked directly in my eyes, lean backed in his chair, put his feet on his desk, and smiled and said "Nunchaku relax, why so serious?" I smiled as well, relaxed, then sat down in the chair behind me. SPC Baker sat down in the chair behind him as well. SGM Julian replied with "Who is your friend?" "This is SPC Baker SGM. He is the person who is allowing me to switch with him to deploy" I stated. "SPC Baker, this is SGM Julian he was my old 1sgt in A.I.T." I added. SGM Julian said "Good to meet you SPC Baker, so you are letting good ole nunchucks switch with you huh?" "Yes" replied "SPC Baker" "Did he tell you how he got the nickname nunchucks?" SGM Julian responded. "No SGM," said SPC Baker "Nunchaku! Exclaimed SGM Julian, "When you have a nickname you are supposed to let people know." "Roger that SGM" I replied.

SGM Julian granted me permission to switch and deploy in place of SPC Baker. We were both elated, and I never told SPC Baker how I got the nickname.

The value of Education

Education is priceless, through my career and my life I have made countless amounts of sacrifices to achieve education or wisdom to reach the next level in life. I joined the Army with an ASVAB a GT score of an 86 after taking the test in ninth grade. After I graduated, I desired to retake the test. While in Iraq, I signed up for Fast Class to retake the ASVAB test. My days in Iraq consist of me conducting a 12-hour shift on Division main. Afterwards, I would walk to Camp Victory to take College Classes even after mortar attacks. The sacrifice was indeed worth it, after completing the class, I would later retake and pass the ASVAB with a 116 GT score. Immediately the Army offered me more job positions and bonuses. My days in Iraq during wartime possessed its own challenges and fun. From flying in a helicopter with the team to Al-Assad, Iraq to road convoys through the Green Zone. While I was five months into my tour in Iraq, I completed paying back my bonus to the Army Reserve. I reported to finance to sign the paperwork to receive my full check in the Army. I enter into the finance department in Iraq very excited to finally receive my first full check since joining Army Active duty. I approached the lady at the window. "My name is SPC Nunnally and I have paid back my debt to Army Reserve." I stated now a newly promoted SPC (Specialist E-4). "Nunnally, if we knew you were on Active Duty Status we would've waive your debt." She replied. I just smiled and walked off. True Story

Upon deploying to Iraq and returning back to Wiesbaden I changed duty stations to Kaiserslautern, Germany. Although, it proved to be a little slow there, it was still fun. I stayed on ROB in Kaiserslautern, Germany, for four months before returning to the United States and being stationed to El Paso, Texas, Fort Bliss.

Life has a funny way of foreshadowing life in its own little way, pay attention to the signs. In each trial we obtain experience, it is through experience we obtain wisdom. You can only achieve wisdom through experience, whether it's yours or someone else's. Business, like life requires wisdom for survival. Business smarts can teach you how to make money however, its wisdom that teaches you business development, how to grow the company, what to invest in, which project is good for the company, which company is good for the company as for as partnerships and mergers, and how to manage company funds. Those successful companies then grow into being successful in their countries. Increasing the countries GDP for the betterment of the citizens. Wisdom is the natural building block of all things; the bible say God created the Earth with wisdom (proverbs 3:19).

Nevertheless, in Fort Bliss, I was again given responsibilities upon arrival. I was placed in charge of the section and the barracks under my First Sergeant Mathuselah. It was an honorable but overwhelming task, due to variety of emergency and disastrous phone calls that I would receive at night from my First Sergeant. My duty in this position was Damage Control. The calls would relate to instances involving soldier's drinking and driving, soldiers fighting with their spouse, needing a cooling off period in the barracks. I would interject diplomatically. Challenges came when I became aware of growing fad and the epidemic that involved soldiers snorting bath salts.

My most difficult account with this occurred for me when we learned of a soldier who snorted bath salts to get high. He placed his newborn baby in the bathtub to bathe her. He let the water run and went back to the living room to continue getting high and playing video games. Afterwards, he fell asleep and took a nap. When he arose, his life would change forever. He still heard the water from the bathroom tub. He remembered his daughter and ran into the bathroom. However, it was too late. His daughter drowned while he was sleep. We were shocked. Upon his arrival to the barrack, I understood the complexities of his mental state at the time. I handled that situation with extreme delicacy as he was already under punitive action by the Army. The Military went to notify his wife of the death of her child due to her husband's neglect and negligence. We were all horrified with the death of an innocent child. I am certain no amount money could bring back the life of his child nor reverse his decision.

This experience subconsciously motivated me to continue the process of being reclassified for a new job and position within the United States Army. I had hopes on going Military Intelligence with my new GT Score. The Army General Classification examination review required me to have a 110 GT score for the MOS (Military Occupation Specialty) I desired which was 35L (Counterintelligence Agent). My GT score is high enough and I proudly have a Secret Clearance "why not?", I thought to myself. Moreover, I found out that the signing bonus for joining Military Intelligence was $40,000. I was informed training would take place in Arizona. I signed up immediately to begin my official reclassification process, but then April 1, 2012, would forever change my plans and my future in the United States Army.

The night of April 1st 2012, I was standing outside of a nightclub with two of my male friends, Levi, and Mark. While we were outside, a man jumped out his car and started yelling at one of my friends I was standing with. Mark told us to just stay calm, that he would go talk to the guy in order to find out what the issue was. Right away, they started wrestling, and they immediately started to fight. Out of nowhere and ever so unexpectedly, the guy pulled out a gun, pointed it at Mark fired one shot hitting him in the chest. Afterwards, he instantly took off running and sped off in his car as Mark laid on the floor, wounded, bleeding and dying. Still in shock and temporarily frozen from the disbelief of what just unfolded, I remember coming back to reality from the screams, shrill, and panic from everyone running from the outside parking lot as they attempted to find safety indoors. I quickly ran to Mark, and attempted to control the bleeding, like we were taught in the Army hoping that it would buy him time before the paramedics arrived. My other friends said it was closer to just drive I loaded him into the car, and we sped toward the hospital emergency room. Yet, he would pass away on route there and was pronounced dead upon arrival. That event would forever change my life and my future in the Army. As I looked down, I saw that I had Mark's blood all over me from the top of my shirt collar down to my shoes. I used a phone to call my First Sergeant and report to him about a tragedy that just unfolded a few moments earlier. When my First Sergeant arrived at the police station where we all went to give our statements and accounts of what occurred at the scene, I called my dear friend, and we rode back together to post. The shooter was caught and sentence to 35 years in prison. Such a senseless and hateful crime, for a reason that didn't equate to an unsuspecting taking of a young man's life.

The next day I was in charge of Physical Training formation. Which meant, I would be in charge of over thirty of America's finest and toughest soldiers for physical fitness, a few hours after a gentleman passed away in my arms. Not surprisingly, I had difficulty sleeping and had several bad dreams that night. Nevertheless, I am disciplined, physically, and mentally tough, trained and proficient in my warrior task and drills.   I've always lived a life of making sacrifices for others and didn't see the difference in that moment regardless of the distress, fear and anger that I was clearly experiencing and internally battling. I was still managing my responsibilities to the soldier's perseverance and determination. At that moment in time the members of the barracks and my section was the most important thing to me. I placed their needs above my own. I still helped the soldiers with their pay and still watch over them in the bay even during my own battles. It wasn't the pay that made me wake up in the middle of the night, to talk to soldiers who wanted to take their life due to situations they found out that happened back home. It was at a young age, I witnessed with my eyes the monstrosities of death, in turn I value life more. After watching a man pass away in your arms, your perception pertaining regarding adults will change. You will begin to identify the innocence in them, as though they are children just looking for safe passage and guidance in life.

Standing in formation I remember hearing my 1SGT call me to the front. "SPC Nunnally, report to the front!" yelled 1SGT. "Moving 1SGT!", I escaped from my thoughts and sounded off. I ran to 1SGT and rendered a salute. "SPC Nunnally, we are doing a battalion run today, run your section" said "1SGT. "Roger that, I replied". As I looked at all the faces staring at me, waiting for me to give an order. I only saw faces of people who weren't aware of the assistance from what they were normally accustomed to. Any mundane discrepancies in which one would normally be conscious of, (typos, on paperwork, missing leave forms, being late to formation etc.) I knew what they really needed assistances with was understanding the value of life. I wanted to yell at the soldiers: "How much money does it take to bring back a life?", I thought. If you knew your brother, sister, husband, wife, child's mother, child's father, or your child was going to pass away tomorrow how much money will you spend to save their life? Would you spend one million dollars to save your mother's life? You will value life over money.

Even with the internal storm and war that I was fighting within myself; one of my Sergeant's believed my grieving period for Mark was a great opportunity to progress his hidden agenda to remove me from the Army by any means. His vendetta was due to him not performing at the same peak as me, my records detailed. For some unexplainable reason, my previous act of assisting a soldier who had discrepancy issues with their salary and pay, somehow enraged him and led him to believe that I was a thorn in his side when I was trying to assist.

It began by him writing fraudulent, forged and frivolous counseling statements about me, which were analogous to insubordinate or infraction statements, in order to demonstrate that I was a delinquent and bad investment for the Army. The problem with his target plan, was that he didn't anticipate that forging my name on these same documents would expose his agenda. When he forged my signature, not only did he also spell my name wrong, but he signed it in a way that wasn't closely similar to my actual signature.

After his narrative that I was personally responsible for the murder of my friend Mark wasn't sticking to those he would disparaging and defaming me to, he settled on telling others that even if I didn't actually kill him that I was responsible for my friend's death. This version and his account of getting others to see me as a thug and threat to the Army caught the attention of some of the other Sergeants, who recommended that I go meet with the Army's Chaplain and tell him everything that happened the night of the murder. What they also did behind my back, was immorally and illegally approach the Chaplain to require him to report back everything that I would share with him our prayer and confessional session.

Yet, with God, fate and righteousness on my side, what the 'Wolfpack" didn't plan for when implementing their hateful plan was the fact that I personally knew the Chaplain from when we deployed in Iraq together, years prior! Rightfully so, when the Chaplain informed me what the Sergeants were planning behind closed doors, I was shocked, hurt and confused and decided to exercise the Army's open-door policy and requested to see the Division's Command Sergeant Major or CSM.

Of course, the chain of command made sure to come to my meeting scheduled with the CSM against regulation. Now with a full audience, brazenly at the meeting standing before me, in my presence. In response, I respectively asked my CSM, "If I was such a bad soldier and a terrible person that they are frivolously trying to convince you that I am, why do I hold these current positions of responsibility since joining the Army, without any prior infractions on my record, Command Sergeant Major?" At 22 years old acknowledgments, included 12 awards, 13 coins, and a waiver for promotion every single year, since enlisting in charge of the barracks and in a E-5 position as a E-4. I explained to him that this was simply the work of one person's resentment and personal vendetta against me that this was some sort of witch hunt. I would come to discourteously refer to those malicious and manipulative

Sergeants as the infamous, "wolfpack" and who God warned me about in scripture since reading the Bible as a child which God provides in Matthew 10:16, "Behold I send you forth as sheep in the midst of 'wolves', so therefore be wise as a serpent, and as harmless as doves".

It is no wonder that all my trials have not suppressed me, for it is the constant word of the Lord that has ordered my steps and allowed me to keep my integrity and morals even in the face of superfluous persecution and adversity.

I was excited to say the least, when CSM Joseph looked me square in the eyes and told me that if I wanted to stay in the United States Army, that I would have to go find a soldier with E-6 ranking or higher, to vouch for me and request me to stay in the Army. Here I found myself having to prove to the Army why it should let me stay in it, no worries, my old unit who was in charge of the post whom I deployed will be sufficient. Nevertheless, irrespective of the fact that outside a missing room key, the night Mark died, I had no prior infractions on my record.

Nonetheless, even if it wasn't fair, I knew that I had to at least fight for the integrity behind my name and all the hard work that I sowed during my time in the military. I wasn't going to just take anyone wrongfully disparaging and accusing me without standing up for myself. I was no longer the small boy frightened at home from the physical abuse from a family member, or the new enlistee being racially discriminated and made to stand in the snow in Germany without appropriate clothing, in order to haze and punish me. I was a proud United States Soldier, and I was Army Strong! However unfair, I was determined to find an E-6 that could vouch for me to submit my 'request to stay in the US Army' letter.

I spoke to Master Sergeant Ruiz (or MSG), who was over strength management for the whole post. He was CSM Joseph's colleague and he knew me personally. I asked him if he could write the letter requested by CSM Joseph via direct email and he emailed CSM Joseph immediately. CSM Joseph told me that he spoke to MSG Aaron. Upon learning the truth, he stated he would let me know of his final decision upon his return from Qatar. Yet, his sudden absence from base only proved to accelerate and expedited the scheming plans of the Sergeants or the "wolfpack", who would use my being lost and my inability to lock the barrack's door, as a conduit to call me unfit to be in the United States Army. Ironically, as per my penchant for following protocol, I am the one that took the initiative to go to my First Sergeant Judeas to report that my key was missing. He is the one that deceptively assured me that a new key was to be ordered for me and would take a few weeks. In the interim, protocol required him to provide me with a memorandum detailing my request for a replacement key and my inability to lock the door to the barracks, something that was required by Army regulations. Yet, instead of giving me a memorandum and filing it in my records, what he instead did was order a barracks inspection knowing that it was impossible to lock the barracks door without a key I just requested the day before and would then list this as a serious infraction that warranted his having to write me up in a counseling statement, along with his official request to have me chaptered our and immediately removed from the army.

In an unbelievable twist of events, he was able to convince another Colonel from outside of my unit to sign my Chapter Packet before CSM Joseph returned from Qatar to challenge this, and with the stroke of that unknown Colonel's pen and his ensuing signature in one instance I was officially chaptered out of the military under the fraudulent assertions that I displayed patterns of misconduct, supported by me leaving my barracks door unlocked once.

The Captain came to me after she found out the truth and she said "Nunnally, I found out the truth I apologize for everything. Do you want to stay in the Army?" I told her I lost faith in the Army and to send me home. Looking back at the decision I do not regret it. Nevertheless, do understand in life, normally, it is right before you quit that a helping hand is given; when you finally realize you cannot do it on your own and you yourself are out of options.

In the end, I was chaptered out the United States Army. I, as an E-4 with my promotable status and security clearance, which is still proudly brandished on my records and which in itself would be deemed an oxymoron for a soldier to have a promotable, high-ranking status if he was deemed to be a delinquent and unequipped to be in a member of the United States Army. Nonetheless, it was impossible to continue a fight in which those you were fighting for were the ones spearheading your demise. One day a great friend of mine from the Army named Benjamin and I were having a discussion. "Nunnally," said Benjamin "you were chaptered out the Army and had the pay back the $30,000." He stated. "Do you believe you should've stayed in Atlanta with the $30,000 in the Army Reserve? He asked. "No", I answered. The experiences I experienced, the people like you who I met along the way, the nights in Germany, and we had the days in Iraq. Thirty-thousand dollars could not buy us five years of consistent, organic, and genuine fun," I told him. I continued to tell him: "Always remember success attracts jealousy. When people are jealous pray for them. Pray they focus on their shortcomings and not your success. The Army taught me the power of the majority shareholder and the pen. The only person who is always right is the Majority Shareholder which is the position I hold today. Always reach for Majority Shareholder," I informed him.

Chapter 6

"I Can Only Go Up … from Here."

After leaving the Army I moved to Illinois and in processed at the VA (Veteran Affairs) in Chicago. While I was there, a gentleman approached me and asked me normal questions. "What branch did you serve in?" he asked. "I was in the Army" I stated. "Are you from Illinois?" he asked, "No I am from Atlanta I stay local, what about you?" I asked him. He informed me he lived in the VA and he was homeless. He was 23 years old. Upon him returning back from the military his parents passed away. He did not have anyone to stay with until he "got on his feet". He stayed in the VA temporarily. Upon hearing the story, I started a nonprofit 501

(C)(3) called "Return to Duty of America" to house homeless veterans then I moved back to Georgia.

Upon moving back to Georgia from Illinois, I called my Mother to let her know I was coming home. Since my enlistment, my daughter was born, and I am a proud Father of a beautiful baby girl. I wanted to be close to my Mother, which would allow her to have the endless opportunity of spending time with her granddaughter. She would be in her upbringing and during her formative years, as the matriarch in her life. Proverbs 17:6 provides that, "Grandchildren are the crown to the elderly…"! That would also allow me to grow the nonprofit. My mother told me that she was living in a city called McDonough, located in Henry County, Georgia. I called my sister and asked her to find me a home that was close to my Mother.

When I arrived in Georgia in 2016, with a new perception of life. I figured I would volunteer more. My mother was excited and she moved in with me. This would alleviate my mind, as I was still battling Mark's demise and how I exited the Army. Businesses fail not because of lack of funding, but businesses fail because of bad partnerships leadership, which then creates a lack of funding. Knowing this I decided to join the Henry County Chamber of Commerce for my Non-profit. I started working on the Government Affairs Committee and I became a Business Ambassador for the Chamber of Commerce. Fortunately for me, when tragedy or loss occurs in my life, I deal with it behind the scenes and stick my head into business until the storm passes. It was during that time I met a young woman name Mrs. Deborah.

Deborah was running for Office I met her at a ribbon cutting. She asked me where I lived, and I told her that I stayed in Henry County. She asked me to visit her Office the next day. I met with her at her office, and after speaking for hours by the time I left her office, I agreed and accepted to join her campaign trail. We went everywhere together; she would call me for campaign trail responsibilities which would help me to get me out my depressive states and moods I was battling. We knocked on doors for her campaign and it worked! I can still hear her calls. "Simeon," she would say. "Yes, Mrs. Deborah" I would reply. "Let's go knock doors!" she would say vigorously. One thing about me is that I did not like to revel in pity and would always opt for the opportunity to put my time towards a good cause for a greater purpose other than myself. Helping her quest to serve the community is how she helped me so much.

Along the way, I would be exposed to an unpredictable world of politics, and we would meet such important figures in history, whose names truly preceded them, such as: Jason Carter, Former President Jimmy Carter's son, and the late Former Congressman John Lewis. It was an unforgettable experience and the best version of what a distraction could afford me during those hard times and hard trials in my life. I would never forget the kindness and camaraderie of Deborah. As God would bless us and fate would smile upon Deborah, she would later go on to win the election. In turn, she would further give me purpose by surprisingly appointing me as Zoning Advisory Board representative.

After being on the Zoning Advisory Board I would then join the National Small Business Association (NSBA), which covered Congressional District 13. I joined the tax committee, the economic development committee, and the technology committee. I met a gentleman, who to this day I still work with. His name was Mr.

Maccabees, or Mr. "Mac", for short. He comes from a long line of legacy as his dad was the second black man to pass the Bar Exam, in the State of Delaware and was singlehandedly accredited with desegregating the State. Mr. Maccabees asked me to join his company and cover the State of Georgia which I agreed. Upon my working with him, he sent me over to the World Trade Center in Atlanta. We conducted his ribbon ceremony at a Country Club in Georgia, and we were off to the races. I smiled in remembrance of such exciting times. After opening his Drone School in Stockbridge, Georgia we aimed next for the city of Warner Robins.

Meanwhile, my colleagues at another major Organization I worked for were so pleased with my performance, that the President would nominate me join the board as the, Youngest ever, Vice President of Business Development for the Organization. It was my job to assist in the growth and development of the entity. I was sworn in as the Vice President of Business Development for the entity. I managed to make some great headway with leaders of a major entity in D.C. I was still flying back and forth to the Democratic Republic of Congo and Dubai as well, working on an infrastructure and development project there.

My mother visited my house one day while I was in Henry County, Georgia. She pulled into the driveway and entered my house since she still had her door key. "Hey Simeon" she said, "Hey Madre," I said she replied with, "Simeon, ummmm" in the softest of voices. Kid like almost so I knew she wanted something. "Yes, Madre," I said with a smile "Can you move in with me?" she asked? "Madre, I am too old for that love." I replied. "Please, I want to pay off my car sooner and we can spend a lot of time together." She insisted. "Let me think about it, Madre." I stated. "That is all I wanted." She said and she left. The next day I called one of my colleagues for a golf game. We went to play golf at one of his golf course developments his name is Joseph (he endorsed the book in the front of the page) I call him Mr. Williams. We went to play golf the following day. While we were on the fourth hole, I said to him, "Mr. Williams, I have an interesting question to ask you." "Yes sir," he responded (Mr. Williams called everyone sir and ma'am. I did not feel important at all.) "My mother asked me to move in with her yesterday. I do not think it is a good idea," I informed him. "Simeon, you have one mother and I wish I could see my mother." He stated. "You're right." I said. "I guess I can look at it as starting over," I said. Then it was my turn, my swing and I asked for silence on the golf course. We continued to play golf and I returned home after a game of golf that day.

The next day I called my mother and told her I would move in with her. At first, I was embarrassed, until three months in staying with her she would give me heavy news.

Upon my return from the Democratic Republic of Congo, a mutual friend introduced me to my future wife at the time, whose name was Sydney. We hit it off right away and we enjoyed each other's company. I was a guest speaker on a World Investment Seminar and of course, I asked my Mother to tune in to watch, as it would be my first time being interviewed on the global stage.

I met a young lady who was also a member of our panel as well and she wanted to introduce me to some of the members of the Royal Office upon my arrival in Dubai. I met her in Dubai, and we went straight to the Royal Office the following day, which turned out to be a truly huge blessing. I immediately called the young lady I was engaged to at the time.

Although I knew that a lot of these roles would be voluntary and uncompensated positions, I was undeterred knowing everything was for the greater good. Not to mention, more enjoyable, was the experience gained along the way. In the end, I later learned that I actually was also given the opportunity to receive compensation after my successful brokering of a deal. I was so excited, learning that God was allowing me to help and feed various people in different regions and countries, while helping to increase the GDP of that country, and in turn the quality of life for its citizens. This reminded me of Proverbs 22:1, that I read, "A good name is to be chosen rather than great riches, loving favor rather than silver and gold".

Now three months into staying with my mother, I went to the cabins for the weekend in North, Georgia. Upon returning from the cabins my mother called me upstairs to her room. "Simeon", she stated. "Yes Madre," I responded. As I walked up the stairs to her huge master bedroom. She was sitting on her bed when I entered. "Yes Madre," I stated again. "Close my door son." She said in a serious voice. "I am diagnosed with breast cancer." I immediately used naivety to cope with the situation. "I will be fine Simeon. God has me if it's time to go it's time to go, and if he heals me, he heals me," She said. "But I have chosen not to take Chemotherapy because it kills more people than it saves. I will not be bound to a death bed. If cancer is going to take me, then so be it, but I will live my life to the fullest extent worshipping my God Ahayah." She replied. "Yes, Madre. We will get through this together. No matter what," I stated in naivety. "I know Simeon." I walked downstairs and entered by room and closed the door and cried. The only person at the time I was aware who had cancer was my mother's mom. She passed away from brain cancer in 1996.

I was no longer embarrassed anymore by moving in with my mother. I knew I was spending more time with her than if I had stayed in my old house. I thank God for allowing me the additional time, memories, and experiences with my mother those moments money cannot buy.

True to form during any major crisis I choose to bury myself in work. Upon working with a major organization, I met a lady who turned out to be an Honorary Consul General. I asked her if I could work with her, and she was very excited. She agreed in giving me the opportunity and a fellowship position within her office. In turn, while at lunch one afternoon, the Consul General would in turn surprise me by saying that she would like to officially appoint me as the Distinguished Fellow in her office. The only person who was at my spontaneous appointment ceremony was Mr. Larry, a CEO of a prestigious investment group in Georgia. I invited him to lunch with Her Excellency and I that day, and we both witness a great moment and great opportunity for me, as I accepted the Fellow offer and began my journey with the Honorary Consul to assist her with issuing Visas on behalf of the Liberian community.

The Consul and I went everywhere together, similar to Mrs. Deborah and me. It was through her teaching me all that she knew and exposing me to the exciting new world of Foreign Policy and Diplomacy. I was able to get a first-row seat into the world of Diplomacy and the Diplomatic Core of Atlanta.

What I immediately observed was that in stark contrast the Diplomatic Core was. It is much more laidback and much more peaceful than that of the political arenas and circles, which just a few years ago, I found myself intrigued by. It is during my time with the Consul, that I would be humbly introduced to a great and honorable, Ambassador, along with all the Ambassadors and Consul Generals from the 73 different Countries, represented here in Atlanta.

I felt such pride in being able to share these once in a lifetime experiences with my Mother. We were extremely supportive and excited for the new world I was delving more and more into, along with the fact that I could really make a big difference in the lives of the people. The Consul General passionately worked on establishing direct air flights from Hartsfield-Jackson Airport to Monrovia, Liberia, as well as the opening of a sister port agreement between Savannah, Georgia and Monrovia. Outside of work and diplomacy life, I excitedly have a new wife and a baby on the way. My career was taking off, and in addition, because of my introduction to the CEO of the Royal Office during my trip to Dubai, he would later appoint me as his Global Trade and Commodities Director. In addition, the Senator of Grand Kru County in Liberia would appoint me to be his Foreign Relations Coordinator, charged with globally representing his office.

Chapter 7
"Joy Attracts … Pain."

Just like success attracts enemies … I believe that joy somehow attracts pain! In the end, we chase money for various forms of ideas which represent our aspirations and acceptance of this sort of attainable social status and familial support. Again, if we achieve all the money in the world, how can we even be certain joy will somehow be presumed to follow? If you can remember the highest point of joy thus far in your life, I'm certain you can remember what happened at the point in time to hurt you the most, possibly just before or soon after experiencing that joy.

I remember the day I landed in Dubai, very vividly and in awe of the innovativeness, beauty, architecture, culture and landscapes that surrounded me. My host received me at his beautiful home, and I was greeted with immaculate hospitality. Ironically, it was upon arrival that I would also receive a letter of good news from the Senator in Liberia, informing me that he would like to prestigiously appoint me as his own personal Foreign Coordinator. Everything should have been lining up, but my Mother's battle and pain was never too far from my mind or too far from my heart. It was impossible for me to revel in every smile, finish every laugh, and respond to every touch when I could see the agony on her face when video calling her at night and when I could see that her strength was dwindling, more and more each day. Yet, as I learned in my childhood and in the Army, you have to show up no matter what the circumstances and get the job done. It was my self-training and perseverance over the years and childhood, along with my military training and faith in God, that would equip me the tools, courage, wisdom and strength to perform and keep going ... while knowing deep down that my Mother was slowly transitioning from the world.

One would think that I would be exceptionally happy and experiencing countless moments of joy as my career was taking off and I had just received appointments from two different Foreign Government Offices. Soon after learning of my Mom's Stage 4 cancer diagnosis, my wife and I got into an explosive fight, which led me to file for a divorce months before my trip to Dubai. It is my wife's phone call to me while overseas, reminding us of our final court date to officiate the divorce, that made me realize that whatever we fought about would not be worth the ending of a marriage and friendship riddled with hardships and pains, outside of our home.

I decided to fly back home to share with her my willingness and eagerness to start all over and focus on the love, intimacy, laughter, and friendship that brought us together in the first place. All the bickering (back and forth) noted during those previous months when tensions were high, and morale was low at home. It only meant we were human and still teaching each another how to maneuver through the throngs of marriage, without any matriarchal or patriarchal guidance to assist us while in the fold and thick of our marital issues.

As soon as I landed back to Atlanta, Georgia, I got home to shower, get dressed, said a silent prayer for strength and then jumped into my vehicle, determined to drive straight from Atlanta, Georgia to Warner Robins, Georgia, in hopes of coming face-to-face with my wife. Sincerely talking about how we could save our marriage and to cancel our divorce proceedings, which was only a mere 72 hours away, or three days' time at that moment. I knew I needed a miracle on my side and knew I possibly would need every one of the advocates in our lives, that I knew would want to see our marriage be successful and fruitful and who would not support our ideas of divorce or our giving up on one another.

While driving, I called one of our mutual friends, Erica, who was actually the one that introduced us, to ask if she could let us borrow her home and if she could get my wife to her house to give us a neutral place to meet and talk. I also, made sure to tag my sister Esdras into help me, by having her call my wife and letting her know that I would be driving to Warner Robbins to see her and to talk to her before our divorce hearing. I knew that this moment was a big deal and whatever happened would ultimately determine whether or not I would be able to fix things with my wife and save our marriage. I wanted to keep my marriage. I didn't want to lose my friend and one of my ribs. I drove faster, ever more determined that this was the right thing to do. As with everything else in my life, this time I had to fight for my chance in love, happiness, joy and family.

I slowed down when I turned into our friend Erica's neighborhood and pulled up in front of her house. I took a deep breath, said a silent prayer, got out of the car and walked up to the door, held my breath and rang the doorbell. Nothing! I waited for a few seconds and rang the doorbell and knocked on the door a few times. Silence! I waited for a little while longer and saw that there was no movement from inside of the house. No one was there. All I received was silence. While walking back to my car I received a single text notification.

I got back into the driver's seat and saw that my wife sent me a single text saying, she was not interested in continuing in our marriage and that she went ahead and has scheduled our final divorce hearing in three days' time. Nothing that I could do to change her mind, and she was sticking with it. A pain shot through me and the idea of losing two women I loved, in such two different drastic and final ways, was just too much for me to bear. I tried calling her, but she would not answer my call. I guess the opportunity to talk and fix our marriage had already passed. I started my car and made the long drive back to Atlanta, as only the sound of the highway, passing cars and the gravel being the only noise surrounding me. Again…joy and pain!

The morning of my final divorce proceeding was a gloomy one. I almost robotically knew what I had to do and where I had to be but was somber and saddened by what I knew may very well be inevitable. I made my way toward the county's divorce court and parked my car in the visitor parking lot. I subconsciously grabbed a parking ticket to store on my dash, unaware of how long it would take to park when one's marriage was ultimately coming to an end. As is customary, I went through the court's metal detector at its entrance before one of the officers assisted me in finding the room and the Judge would be proceeding over our matter.

When I walked in and saw my wife, Samantha, sitting in the room waiting for the proceedings to begin, my heart leaped into my throat, and I called her name to look at me and asked her to give us a private moment to talk. I begged her not to go through with the divorce, but she already had her mind made up and calmly replied to me that, "People got remarried all of the time" she said. "Remarried?" I stated, "Why do we need to be remarried, if we just don't get divorced in the first place?" I added. My mind was blown, my heart confused, and my spirit was tired. My Mom was even more sick than she was a few days ago and on her death bed. It was all too much, but together I knew that with God, we could fight this and fix us, if she was willing to take that leap of faith again and make true to our vows, because in the end … we were only standing in a court room because of an irrelevant argument, that went too far. My wife agreed after hearing this and admitted that we did in fact have more good days than bad days.

When the presiding Judge, came into the room, after we were allowed the time to speak privately just amongst ourselves as a couple, she turned to my wife and asked her how she would like to move forward regarding the divorce proceedings. She looked the Judge straight in her eyes, using the most regal voice she could muster, and calmly stated that she would like to finalize our divorce. The judge granted the divorce, I signed the required documents as required by the courts. We both got into our own separate cars, and we drove away no longer a unit.

Married couples, what is greater than meeting someone? Falling in love with them and getting married. Having a beautiful wedding and a beautiful child. Every day you wake up, you see the half of yourself and half of your spouse in the embalmment of genuine love. What is more fulfilling? When problems arise speak with your spouse or other married friends. No one wants to transition to heaven alone. Do not let bad advice from outsiders cause you to lose the person you love. That is foolish. My situation was different nevertheless, do not let people talk you into making choices in their relationship that they would not do themselves. Value your relationship.

When you pass away, people will reflect on how good of a person you were, how well you treated others, how much they dedicated themselves to their family, the wisdom they demonstrated, and whether they ultimately believed in God.

Enriching your own quality of life and the lives of others, through the consistent and constant acts of kindness, fellowship, milestone moments, support, and a million days filled with memories and love that would rival any of Midas' treasure troves. In the end, objects only attract objects and life attracts life, objects cannot attract life. Meaning, money can only be valued by the kind of object it attracts, yet people are valued by the type of people they attract and keep in their lives.

Life is like climbing a mountain blindfolded and inexperience. While climbing, you hope to reach the top of the mountain not knowing where you are going or when you will experience triumph, knowing deep down that you don't have all the tools necessary for the climb and the road ahead is unprecedented and unknown. Being blindfolded means, you are unaware of any dangers to look out for while on this quest, yet, admitting that you are conditioning yourself and learning new skillsets and life lessons as you climb, thus learning from your mistakes, along the way. Yet, because our tour guide is God and the Holy Spirit, our optimism, grit and determination is actually powered by our faith and principles. We look toward the sky and realize that looking back and looking down isn't an option, and that we can "only go up from here".

Regardless of our trials and strife on how much we have endured, all that has happened to us, we channel our ability to focus these life lessons to be therapeutic and motivational, as reminders, testaments, and literal guides throughout our life for others. Thus, every loss or betrayal becomes understandably a necessary lesson, regardless of how much pain it has caused and how long the throbbing within my heart and soul gnaws and lingers. Angels become friends and guides, and what was once maybe considered a justification of their loyalty, instead becomes a new version of something more valuable than gold.

Success then becomes a new goal, not because of greed, but because of the desire to demonstrate the attainment of triumph and the testament of survival. Regardless of how many cuts you endure, how many times you drop your spike, how many times you slip your footings, how many times you accidentally miscalculated your next move you will keep going. God is with you always. He will answer your prayers as per the purpose for the life that he has already inscribed for you at your inception. So, you keep learning, keep moving, and keep asking God to navigate your path; irrespective of the obstacles that may arise, and the ability to stay focus and the courage necessary to not give up.

Every mountain has a peak we were not made to have peaks, regardless of how you feel mentally, spiritually, emotionally, and physically giving up is not an option and perseverance is used to light your way. Make sure you're climbing the mountain of happiness and love, not greed, greed can never be satisfied.

Chapter 8

This Balance Called Life

I made the decision to move to Gwinnett County to be closer to my Mother to be able to help out as much I could with her care.

Personally, and professionally, those days were riddled with stress, challenges and proved immensely taxing on my spirit. I tried to be tough and keep a brave exterior, while dealing with the absence of my wife and the unknown time of my mother's transition. Yet, I knew as a CEO, and newly appointed to two International Government Offices, I couldn't let my company nor the people in the countries be impacted by the personal strife I was experiencing, behind closed doors. I attempted to take a four-month hiatus until the month of April, which never materialized, and which proved futile.

The month of April came however, and the 1st of the month which I've come to dread due to the it being the anniversary of Mark's shooting and murder, was enough to unseat me, but I kept strong because my Mother needed me to be strong for her. On the 2nd of April, it seems that life would give me another curveball, when my Mother called me and in the faintest of voices, "Simeon." Said Madre "Yes Madre" I said. "Are you coming to see me today?" she asked me. I told her, "Absolutely, I will be there right away!"

When I arrived to a family member's house, where my Mom poignantly quested to spend her final days, a family member stopped me right before entering my Mom's room, and told me very shakingly but also very sternly, that I needed to prepare myself for what I was about to see. Right away, I blew her off and thought that she was just being dramatic or protective of me before seeing my Mother, but that she also failed to remember that I am an Army veteran and have seen things with my own eyes that I could never describe to another. Yet, no stint in the Army could prepare a Son with the sight of seeing the full deterioration of what cancer does to the body, face, skin, and voice of a Mother that has held them and nurtured them since they were a small child. The Mother that wiped away tears, put bandages on knees, that used her work phone to talk to you when you couldn't sleep at night, the Mother who quit jobs to come to your football games and danced to Toni

Braxton songs while cooking meals on summer days, seemed to be departing.

Yet, the family member was right to heed that warning to me. As soon as I stepped into my Mom's room, I gasped as the sight of her took my breath away. I immediately walked out of the room before she could see my expression of pain and shock and stepped into the closest bathroom to cry my eyes out while making sure to smother my sobs, so no one would hear me. Being strong for others and being there others was very easy for me, and this was my Mother that needed me in these darkest and most final of hours.

I regained my composure, stepped, and went back towards her room. With my hand on the closed doorknob, I took a deep breath and rushed into her room with as much joy and positive energy that I could muster. One thing my Mom knew was that she could depend on me since I was a child, willingness, and incessant attempts to try to make her laugh or giggle uncontrollably. Her sadness was my sadness, her joy was my joy. She was my first love, and I was her last child and her baby boy.

"Madre, it's me, Simeon!" I spoke. "I came to see you, how are feeling today my love", I asked. It was only the strength of God which could make me sound so normal in the looming reality that we were all about to face very soon. My heart was shattering into little pieces within, and I knew that my Mother was beginning her transition. Her complexion was much lighter, breathing was shallow, she was having problems swallowing at this point, her organs were shutting down and her voice barely came out in full whispers, causing the person speaking with her to have to ardently lean in to hear what she was saying, and to also make sure she didn't have to strain herself in frustration to redundantly repeat herself.

Yet, when she replied, "Hi, Simeon, hey my son", my heart melted. I had peace knowing that she knew that I came and that I was here with her and that I wouldn't be leaving her side again, until it was time for her to go home with God. I asked her, if there was anything that I could do for her, and when I saw that she fell back asleep, I made sure to just stay in the room with her arranging whatever I could on her tables and in her bathroom. When I was done with that, and realized that I was fidgeting nervously, I just sat next to her in the chair next to her bed, listening to the sounds of the soft hum of the oxygen tank as it provided oxygen throughout my Mother's failing body and lungs. I was devastated but determined that her last few days on earth wouldn't be one riddled with sorrow or melancholy, but rather music, reading scriptures together as we once did when I was younger, and reminiscing about the good old days.

The human body is an interesting thing. Just two weeks, prior I was with my Mother at a family barbecue at my Aunt's house, and she was speaking, walking around, driving, and shopping. Yet, now in her bedroom holding her tiny hand, I felt her frailty and her tiredness for fighting this disease. Holding my mother's hand, it was weakest hand on the strongest woman I ever knew. This was all moving too fast. I never had the opportunity to come to terms with the fact that my Mother, my everything, was actually sick and transitioning. These last two years, and last few months, specifically, I was just certain that she would holistically beat her cancer as she was determined to and that she would be a perpetual testament and the ultimate survivor. How could someone that I considered the strongest woman I ever met, be unable to barely squeeze my hand or keep her eyes open long enough to converse with me? I was scared… I was heartbroken.

I quietly got out of the chair, making sure not to wake my Mother and creeped slowly out of the room, making sure to close the door as quietly as possible, before rushing down the hallway and back to bathroom. I looked around before stepping inside to allow my emotions to overflow and secretly spill out again in sobs and choked back tears. I prayed for God to give me strength, and to soothe and cover my Mother during her final days to lessen the pain that she was in. I'm not sure how long I stayed in that bathroom crying, but when I was done, I washed my face again and dried it off.

My mother also kept her laugher and her faith in God her last days. I went to her and kissed her one day and she looked at me and said, "Simeon, do not put your wet lips on my skin. My love."

I learned a lot in those last few days of my Mother's life from watching a family member care for her. It was truly an honor to assist in the physical and medical part of caring for her, grooming her, and carrying her. I was the son that she took care of when I was sick, or the son that she would soothe my worries away by making me hot chocolate with extra whip cream, just the way I liked it; and the son that she would surprise with my favorite sweets freshly made, warm honey buns. It was now my turn to nurture and protect her, as she had done for so many years for me. My Army training kicked in while the for my Mother in those last few days became the most important objective and mission of my life. I would receive the assistance of individuals, in both the medical and nursing fields, to contribute in making my Mother feel as comfortable as possible in lieu of the extreme amount of pain she was battling every single time she moved or took a breath. Other friends would call with prayers, some would bring food and essentials over for my family, so we had one less thing to worry about. Those days lent to the testament of community and village, and I was truly grateful for mine! These are moments in life when people start valuing life. At the end, we as people shouldn't wait to the end of someone's life to show compassion or forgive, and what good is money if you are by yourself without family or friends?

A few days later, and still refusing to leave my Mother's side, we were told that the time had come and that it was necessary for my Mother to be transported to an inpatient hospice facility by way of an ambulance ride, due to her organs failing. I didn't want to face what going to a hospice facility meant, but I knew that I had to be there to hold her hand on the long drive there. Also, I knew that I had to be strong for her. Although my Mother lost her ability to speak those last few days and hours of her life, I knew that she could hear my voice and feel my love, and that was enough for me.

The next day, on April 9, 2023, at 10:12am, my Mother would transition in her hospice bed and depart from this world, nine days short of her April 18th birthday. As the machine monitoring her vitals and her heart flatlined, and the hospice equipment began to beep all at the same time, a family member called her name over and over again. My auntie said my mother's name three times "Sonya, Sonya … Sonya", yet my Mother did not reply. She was gone.

My mother was my first idea of a Wife, and truly the First Love of My Life. She is the woman that taught me how to walk, not once, but twice.

She's the one that would hold my arm as we went on our weekend strolls to the park to try to guess the name of the trees we saw. She was the one that I had my first bible study with, and the one that would laugh at my silly and ridiculous jokes that I was always determined to make because the sound of her laughter was music to my ears. The way her beautiful face lit up when she smiled could literally warm up my heart on the coldest of winter days. She was Sonya, she was Madre, she was my Mother…and even now no longer with me. She is still perfect, and I am numb.

As I stood in her now hospice room, emotionless, numb, and unfeeling, I tried to imagine how I would survive this world without her guidance, love, protection, and presence along the lonely paths and roads forcing me involuntarily to go toward the grotesque and painful concept and life without my Mother and the inevitable avoidance in facing alone … these new beginnings.

Chapter 9
Who Really Wants…Money?

Like most I was chasing a foundation of money and status to obtain comforts and provisions for them, were in the end done so in vain … because they were no longer around to see the success aspired to finally cultivate into a reality.

The sacrifices and time lost with my family could never be retraced or replaced. In retrospect, when I was at back-to-back business meetings with a colleague, I could've been at lunch with my Mother, or attempting to learn the humility needed to win my ex-wife back, instead of pleading for a chance for reconciliation in a small divorce court holding room, the day our divorce would be finalized for good.

I should have spent more time reading and studying the Bible to reinforce my role as a Husband, Son, a Father, and a brother. I could have been more to my family, what I was to the world. It didn't matter enough if I was considered a reliable colleague and friend, who would jump to assist anyone, anywhere where I was needed. What good does it do to build my Curriculum Vitae and update my email signature block, if I walked into an empty home every evening and no longer had the option of picking up the phone to hear my Mom's voice, prayers, or laughter.

I realized I wasn't grateful enough and satisfied with the richness that God had already provided me with, that came in the form of Fatherhood, marriage, and family memories. In the end, I lost unalterable time pursuing titles, wealth, and business opportunities. All for what? The bitter taste of money!

I could easily have made time to go on cruises with my Mom, which was something she truly enjoyed, or regrettably so, I could have went on a million more walks with her not chase a million more dollars. Not a day or second goes by, that I don't think about my Mom, who I affectionately called 'Madre'.

As men, we sometimes feel as providers and hunters that the sacrifices that we find ourselves making for our loved ones, warrants our absence, travel, and time away from our families. When in fact, all that we hope to attire … can be found in the middle of the living room in our homes for Taco Tuesdays together, card and game nights on Fridays, bedtime stories and tea parties, passing a football with our sons… and most importantly, flowers on random days not motivated by Holidays only and date nights to remind your love and spouse that they are truly the heartbeat that keeps you going and the compass that leads you home.

The number of things that we lose, knowingly and unknowingly during our hunt for money, success and status, in the end cannot compute to any form of currency or valuation … which is the reason why love is deemed to be inestimable in the first place. It is the one that we cannot purchase, buy, manipulate, lease, rent, leverage or control.

I endeavor to everyone reading this memoir and truly encourage you to seek a happiness that is first premised on God, and then align that love and pray that God discloses to you the purpose he has inscribed for you to follow. In that way, your constant prayer, obedience, discipline, and faith will guide your direct steps as you maneuver through the titles that matter the most … Parent, Spouse, Sibling, Daughter, Son, and Friend. With such simple ways of rethinking life, you will then avoid living with regret when you lose any of the above-mentioned loved ones in your life. For it is the memories that we acquire over the years and the timestamps of love, compassion, and community that will prove perpetually everlasting and powerful and true. The mere chasing of success and wealth for vanity reasons or to prove something to someone else or an ever-changing society, is truly futile and pointless. If you want something to aspire to … aspire for genuine love, sincere contentment, purpose, and legacy.

In the end when you think about it there is a path we can all venture down in which we can achieve wealth, normally it is either with false love, isolation, or a feeling of missing something. The true journey to wealth is through the process of life and living life principles through understanding and wisdom. Self-acceptance is a part of the true value of life. Acceptance of yourself is just as important as acceptance of your life purposes. Wisdom will teach you life, and wisdom will teach you business. When you look at how much you have to sacrifice to obtain it, you will say: "Who really wants money?" Why don't we all reach for wisdom, genuine love from those we genuinely love; joy, God, family, happiness, and the simplicities of life instead.

REBIRTH

I feel like a leaf in the summer breeze
Carrying a seed being blown from the west to the east...
Overseeing the ocean view...
different color spectrums of orange and yellow sunrays...
Excited to be a part of the new tree ....
knowing that it only comes when it's life decays

I feel like the farmer standing outside ...
seeing the storm approach unprovoked
He hides him and his family under the porch ...
calmly telling his kids don't fear the noise
Knowing the storm is violent but well needed
For, if it wasn't for the storm ...
his crops wouldn't have fertilize soil to grow this season

I feel like a virgin loosing her virginity ...
to her husband feeling the pain internally
The bee protecting his family ...
knowing he loose his life instantly after one of his own bee stings
The male spider mating with the black widow...
...dies for the shake of his bloodline
In all cases a sacrifice is made
to continue the circle of life and time

You shed your old ways to let the new you shine...
The circle of life and time is define...
You can only have life when something dies
Even you are here becase someone ...died...

written by...

SIMEON NUNNALLY

Genuine Love

The excitement of achieving gratification after
delay and delay
of emotional frustration and standing up to sexual
temptations
Now giving over your vulnerabilities to the mere
image of one who matches your personality
Comfort your insecurities love, at its genuine purity
Romance is the energy giving into your desires
only when people capitalize on opportunities with
the one they admire,
Putting down their guard believing in the proper
alignment of the stars
Acknowledging their prayers were heard by God
This is the real deal and not a fraud
Finally, I pulled the Ace of spades and not the joker
card
Slow walks on the beach feeling the sand under
your feet
Holding hands watching the sunset, soft kisses on
your lover's neck
Stomach kissing seeing with a clear vision
You finally got what you been missing

The prescription your medicine this love Jones you pop in
Recovering from the domestic lesson from the last adult adolescence
even as adult we learn lessons
Love is better when love, is met with love
Hugs are better when hugs are met with love
You are my destiny means you are my what's meant for me
Now to eternity from now to where I'm destined to be
Only giving to me by the purpose of what's the purpose of me
Foundation for a family love is offense it's no need to be defensive in love
You maybe offended but, don't be offensive in love
Life is well written romance is well scripted
Love give us the rib to our existence, but pride can interfere with that
When two hearts desires match nothing should interfere with that

-Simeon H. Nunnally

Special Thanks

My God I am who I am Ahayah Ashar Ahayah Exodus 3:14 And God said unto Moses, I Am That I Am: and he said, Thus shalt thou say unto the children of Israel, I Am hath sent me unto you. Translate I am that I am into Hebrew it is Ahayah Ashar Ahayah. That is God's true name. Shalom!

My mother, Madre Sonya my love I miss you dearly.
My family
My baby girl my love Shari Mae Nunnally
Multinational African Partners Inc, God's favorite Company.

J.T Williams CEO of Killearn Property a blessing to my life a great mentor business partner and spiritual friend

Ron Hubbard and Cheryl Hubbard and the Multinational African Partners Inc. family God's favorite company

My bosses:

His Excellency Dunston Pereira CEO to the Private Office of HH Sheikh Ahmed Bin Faisal Al Qassimi

Senator Bartekwa Senator Liberia Grand Kru

Representative Eric Bell House District 75 Georgia

Zane Copeland Jr. "also known as" Lil Zane

Erica R. Baker (Florida A&M University) Edits
Glenn Williams
Lacy Anderson
David Augustinvil
Keevan Andrew
Joshua Woomer
Nicolas Balli
501st Military Police Company
World Trade Center Association

Commissioner Dee Clemmons
Super Delegate Richard Ray
Her Excellency Cynthia Blandford Consul General
of Liberia
Her Excellency Dr. Elaine Grant Bryant Consul
General of Jamaica
His Excellency Kevin Casebier Consul General of
Latvia

Mr. Rafiq Ahmed 100 Black Men of South Metro
Atlanta

www.ingramcontent.com/pod-product-compliance
Lightning Source LLC
Chambersburg PA
CBHW050334160726
48002CB00001B/312